Psychology After Psychoanalysis

Ian Parker has been a leading light in the fields of critical and discursive psychology for over 25 years. The *Psychology After Critique* series brings together for the first time his most important papers. Each volume in the series has been prepared by Ian Parker, features a newly written introduction and presents a focused overview of a key topic area.

Psychology After Psychoanalysis is the fourth volume in the series and addresses three important questions:

- Why is psychoanalysis re-emerging within psychology?
- How can psychoanalytic ideas inform psychosocial research?
- How does psychoanalysis explain the relation between the individual and society?

International in scope, the book includes a clear account of psychoanalysis, and the different varieties of the approach that are at work inside and outside the discipline of psychology. It explores the status of psychoanalysis as a series of concepts and as a methodology, and shows how its clinical practice is crucial to the way that it operates now in an academic context. In doing so, the book sheds light on the arguments currently occurring inside psychoanalysis, with discussion of its relation to critical psychology, psychosocial research, the health professions, culture and social theory.

Parker shows how psychoanalysis rests on a notion of 'method' that is very different from mainstream psychology, and unravels the implications of this difference. Early chapters examine the lines of debate between various psychoanalytical traditions, and show how critical psychology challenges the assumptions about human nature and subjectivity made in conventional psychoanalysis. Later chapters introduce the methodological device of 'transference' and explore how psychoanalysis may be utilized as a resource to review key questions of human culture.

Psychology After Psychoanalysis is essential reading for students and researchers in psychology, sociology, social anthropology and cultural studies, and for discourse analysts of different traditions. It will also introduce key ideas and debates in critical psychology for undergraduates and postgraduate students across the social sciences.

Ian Parker is Professor of Management in the School of Management, University of Leicester, UK, Visiting Professor in the Department of Psychosocial Studies, Birkbeck, University of London, and Co-Director of the Discourse Unit, UK (www.discourseunit.com).

Psychology After Critique

Ian Parker has been at the centre of developments in critical and discursive psychology for over 25 years. The *Psychology After Critique* series brings together for the first time his most important and influential papers. Each volume in the series has been prepared by Ian Parker, presents a concise and focused overview of a key topic area, and includes a newly written introduction which traces the continuing impact of the 'crisis', 'deconstruction', 'discourse analysis', 'psychoanalysis' and 'Lacanian research' inside the discipline of psychology.

Volumes in the series:

Psychology After the Crisis
Scientific paradigms and political debate

Psychology After Deconstruction
Erasure and social reconstruction

Psychology After Discourse Analysis
Concepts, methods, critique

Psychology After Psychoanalysis
Psychosocial studies and beyond

Psychology After the Unconscious
From Freud to Lacan

Psychology After Lacan
Connecting the clinic and research

Psychology After Psychoanalysis

Psychosocial studies and beyond

Ian Parker

Routledge
Taylor & Francis Group
LONDON AND NEW YORK

First published 2015
by Routledge
27 Church Road, Hove, East Sussex BN3 2FA

and by Routledge
711 Third Avenue, New York, NY 10017

Routledge is an imprint of the Taylor & Francis Group, an informa business

British Library Cataloguing in Publication Data
A catalogue record for this book is available from the British Library

Library of Congress Cataloging in Publication Data
Parker, Ian, 1956–
Psychology after psychoanalysis : psychosocial studies and beyond / Ian Parker.
pages cm.—(Psychology after critique)
Includes bibliographical references and index.
1. Psychoanalysis. 2. Critical psychology. 3. Social psychology. I. Title.
BF173.P2854 2014
302—dc23
2014006451

ISBN: 978–1–84872–212–5 (hbk)
ISBN: 978–1–84872–213–2 (pbk)
ISBN: 978–1–31577–406–0 (ebk)

Typeset in Times New Roman
by Swales & Willis Ltd, Exeter, Devon

Contents

Series foreword

In the essays collected in these six volumes Ian Parker has brought together for the first time the two radical movements that began in social psychology in the 1960s and 1970s. One of these movements was based on a critical appraisal of the defective methodology of the research programmes that emanated from mainstream American social psychologists. This was rejected for a variety of reasons by a wide variety of critics who shared the belief that people actually deal with what they take to be the meanings of what is happening around them and the significance of the arenas in which actions were performed, according to the rules and conventions of their local social order. The results of a shallow, positivistic approach to discerning the wellsprings of human social behaviour were rejected as sources of reliable knowledge. How people thought, acted, felt and perceived their worlds had little to do with how people actually lived their lives together. People in the stripped-down meaningless worlds of the social psychological experiment were not reacting to stimuli, just trying to make sense of anomic situations with whatever resources their education and history had provided them. People are not empty sites for causal processes but active agents engaged in the tasks and projects that their lives throw up.

At the same time, and for the most part independently, a different kind of criticism was emerging – a display of the moral aspects of the very kind of psychology that was rejected as unscientific by the methodological sceptics. If people believed that psychologists were unearthing the truth about how people thought and acted, then insofar as actual people were unlike this paradigm they would or should strive to achieve it. The realization that such psychology-driven workbooks of human vagaries such as the DSM series of manuals, by presenting a range of ways for human beings to live and act as disorders, defined a kind of person to be emulated who was very much like the bland artefact generated by the statistical methods of the American mainstream, all dissent and difference being ironed out in the deference to some arbitrary level of statistical significance. Critical psychology began to reveal the ways in which the power structures of society and the relations between people from different social classes were brought about. Critical psychology drew from social constructionism the principle that when you can see how something is manufactured you can change it.

The strangest of all the eccentricities of the 'main stream' was the neglect of language. It could hardly be more obvious that the main medium of social interactions is linguistic. Once that is acknowledged the way is open for another dimension – the study of the differences between the linguistically differentiated cultures of the various tribes of humankind. This was not 'cross-cultural psychology' which was merely the transfer of Western middle-class conceptions of life to shape research into the lives of people of very different ways of thinking and acting.

In this elegant introduction to the field of critical psychology Ian Parker shows how gradually but inexorably the two streams began to merge, a process that is continuing. The most striking way in which a critical psychology is currently evolving is in the development of psychology as a moral science. Tied to this insight are explicit studies of the way rights and duties come between natural and acquired tendencies to act and the possibilities that different local moral orders allow: the rapidly growing field of positioning theory.

But all was not plain sailing. The turn to deconstruction, via a reshaping of the linguistic turn to encompass the richer domain of discourse, led to the neglect of the key claim that the 'new psychology' gave socially relative and epoch-specific reliable knowledge, at least pro tem. To reclaim psychiatry from the neurochemists, the place of the active person within a local framework was an essential core to be defended. If persons fade away into clusters of locally contingent selves the key point of the reality of human agency was in danger of being lost.

The second deep insight – perhaps more important than the defence of persons, was relocation of 'mind' to the social network of meaningful interactions, the mind in society. When we learn to abstract ourselves one by one from the social nexus from which each of us emerges we bear with us the indelible mark of our cultural origins. The recoverable content of psycho-dynamics relocates the unconscious to 'what lies between'. In the end we turn back to language and relate symbolic systems not as abstract calculi obeying inbuilt species-specific rules but as the common instruments with which we manage our lives. Psychology can be nothing but the study of cultural-historical-instrumental practices of our ever-changing tribal societies.

The *Psychology After Critique* series is the comprehensive resource we have been waiting for to enable new generations not only of budding psychologists but all those who concern themselves with how we might live, to find their way through the mistakes of the positivistic illusion of a science to a just appreciation of what it might be to come to understand the myriad ways a human being can be a person among persons.

Rom Harré
Linacre College, University of Oxford, UK
Psychology Department, Georgetown University, USA

Series preface

What is psychology? Once upon a time psychologists imagined that they knew the answer to this question. Their object of study, they argued, should be the way that individuals perceive the world, think about it and act in it together with other people. Perception and thinking, in developmental and cognitive psychology, for example, was studied as if it only happened inside the heads of the experimental 'subjects' in scientific laboratories and then 'social psychology' often amounted to little more than an accumulation of the behaviour of those same atomized individuals. The idea that people talked to each other, and that this talk might actually have an effect on the way that people behaved and understood themselves was outside the frame of that kind of academic work.

This series of books is about the consequences of talk being taken seriously, the consequences for scientific investigation and for the way that many researchers today are building innovative new research projects. The discipline of psychology has been transformed since a 'paradigm crisis' erupted nearly half a century ago when pioneers in research into the role of language in thinking and behaviour picked up the thread of early 'radical psychology' critiques which homed in on the limitations of their discipline. The 'paradigm crisis' threw into question the silent world presupposed by the psychologists and launched us all into a world of intense debate over the role of language, of discourse and then of what is shut out of discourse, of the unconscious and of psychoanalysis.

These books were produced in the context of fierce arguments about methods in psychology and over the kinds of concepts we needed to develop in order to do better more radical research. The Discourse Unit was founded in Manchester as a Centre for Qualitative and Theoretical Research on the Reproduction and Transformation of Language, Subjectivity and Practice in 1990. Today it operates as an international trans-institutional collaborative centre which supports a variety of qualitative and theoretical research projects contributing to the development of radical theory and practice. The term 'discourse' is used primarily in critical hermeneutic and structuralist senses to include inquiries influenced by feminism and psychoanalysis. The centre functions as a resource base for qualitative and feminist work, as a support unit for the (re)production of radical academic theory, and as a networking centre for the development of critical perspectives in action research.

We took as our starting point the 'crisis' and the need for critical reflection on the discipline of psychology, the place of psychology and appeals to psychology in other academic disciplines. We then saw the need for a 'critical psychology' that was concerned not only with what went on inside the academic world but also with the way that psychological ideas functioned in the real world outside the universities. The books in this series are written mostly by one individual participant in those debates, but they bring together a number of different arguments for perspectives on the nature of scientific paradigms, deconstruction from literary theory, discourse analysis, psychosocial studies, psychoanalysis and clinical work that were elaborated by researchers in the Discourse Unit.

The books together trace a narrative from the early recognition that language is crucial to understand what is happening in traditional laboratory-experimental psychology – why that kind of psychology is quite useless in telling us about human action – to the development of discourse analysis and the connections with some more radical attempts to 'deconstruct' language from other neighbouring disciplines. A concern with different kinds of psychoanalytic theory – the innovative work now taking place in psychosocial studies – is then introduced to conceptualize the nature of subjectivity. But from the beginning there are some 'red threads' that lead us from the study of language and subjectivity to the study of power and ideology.

These books about psychology as an academic discipline and the increasing role of psychology in our everyday lives are also about the politics of research. And so, when we began to discuss the role of 'deconstruction' or 'psychoanalysis' in the Discourse Unit we always asked whether those other conceptual frameworks would help or hinder us in understanding the connections between knowledge and social change. The books do not pretend to be neutral disinterested description of trends of research in psychology. Our 'crisis' was always about the possibility that the turn to language would also be a turn to more politically engaged – Marxist and feminist – radical reflection on what the theories and methods conceal and what we could open up. The books are accounts of the emergence of key debates after 'the crisis' and sites of 'critical psychological' reflection on the nature of psychology itself.

Ian Parker
Professor of Management in the School of Management,
University of Leicester, and Co-Director of the Discourse Unit
(www.discourseunit.com)

Acknowledgements

This book brings together versions of papers that were either published in scattered places and are often inaccessible or that are unpublished. Chapter 1 was drawn from my 2008 paper 'Psychoanalytic Theory and Psychology: Conditions of Possibility for Clinical and Cultural Practice', *Theory & Psychology*, 18, (2), 147–165, reprinted by permission of Sage Publications Ltd; Chapter 2 was drawn from my 2004 'Psychoanalysis and Critical Psychology', in D. Hook (ed.) *Critical Psychology* (pp. 138–161) published in Cape Town, reprinted here with permission of Juta Press; Chapter 3 was first published in 2010 as 'The Place of Transference in Psychosocial Research', *Journal of Theoretical and Philosophical Psychology*, 30(1), 17–31, copyright © 2010 by the American Psychological Association, reproduced with permission; Chapter 4 was first published in 2012 as 'Freud's culture', in A. Gülerce (ed.) *Re(con)figuring Psychoanalysis: Critical Juxtapositions of the Philosophical, the Sociohistorical and the Political in Our Times* (pp. 45–59), published by and reproduced with permission of Palgrave Macmillan (the full published version of this publication is available from http://us.macmillan.com/reconfiguringpsychoanalysis/AydanGülerce); Chapter 5 was first published in 2006 as 'Losing psychoanalysis in translation', *The Letter: Lacanian Perspectives on Psychoanalysis*, 37, 72–92, reprinted with the permission of the Editorial Board of the journal *The Letter: Irish Journal for Lacanian Psychoanalysis*, as it has been titled since 2008; Chapter 6 was drawn from a much longer paper published in 2012 as 'Žižek, NSK, Marxism, Psychoanalysis and the State: Cynicism and Resistance to Capitalism and Bureaucracy in Europe' by the *International Journal of Žižek Studies*, 6(1). I have modified some formulations in the published papers and excluded extraneous material. I am, as ever, grateful to Erica Burman and my colleagues in the international network around the Discourse Unit for their critical comments and support during the preparation of this volume. The mistakes must surely in some way be theirs too.

Introduction

Psychology after psychoanalysis

This book, Volume 4 of the series *Psychology After Critique*, is about the impact of psychoanalysis on critical debates in psychology, and about the way the 'paradigm crisis' in the discipline passed through a 'turn to language', through a 'turn to discourse' and then to a 'turn to subjectivity' in the rapidly evolving sub-field of 'psychosocial studies'.

This introduction provides an account of key ideas in psychoanalysis, including Freud's work and the way his ideas are usually represented and misunderstood inside psychology today. I will also review some of the different traditions in psychoanalysis that build upon and, in some cases, challenge Freud's assumptions about human nature. The debate between these different psychoanalytic traditions, which is explored in greater detail in the course of the book, is what gives psychosocial studies its lively character and which has enabled it to take forward the 'new paradigm' revolution in the discipline that began back in the late 1960s (Parker, 1989).

When we founded the Discourse Unit in 1990 we were reluctant at first to engage with psychoanalysis because it seemed to us at the time to be a way of interpreting behaviour that repeated many of the worst features of psychology as a discipline, one that has been responsible for defining what is 'normal' and 'abnormal'. We did include psychoanalytic research as one of the four influential 'resources' in our work (along with post-structuralism, feminism and Marxism), but many of us were shy of taking it seriously. Since then some of us have tackled Freud and his followers in more depth, but have still kept it at arm's length, and one way of doing that has been to treat 'psychoanalytic discourse' as a structuring feature of subjectivity in contemporary culture rather than as a universally correct underlying account of human psychology. That is, instead of assuming psychoanalysis is true we look at how it has taken shape as a 'social construction' peculiar to capitalist society.

This book should be read alongside the other books in the series, which explore in more detail the origins of the 'crisis' which facilitated the emergence of qualitative research (in a turn to language) and discourse analysis (as a turn to discursive psychology), and books which then look in detail at Freud's ideas and the work of the French psychoanalyst Jacques Lacan. In this introduction I set the scene for three issues that this book explores. I look at why psychoanalysis is now re-emerging inside psychology, why psychoanalytic ideas are seen as valuable for the development of psychosocial studies, and how psychoanalysis tackles the vexed question of the relation between the individual and society. These issues are critical for any attempt to do justice to the complexity of human psychology and our nature as social beings whose behaviour and experience is intimately connected with others, and they are issues that are central to the development of what has become known as 'critical psychology' (Parker, 1999a, 2011a).

The returns of psychoanalysis

Psychoanalysis is now re-emerging inside psychology, but in a form that is very different from earlier incarnations of the approach in the discipline. There are some kinds of psychoanalysis that are very 'psychological', of course (Kovel, 1974; Cushman, 1991). However, it is often forgotten that psychologists in the early twentieth century took Freud to be one of the founders of psychology, and there were many attempts to build psychological theories of development, personality and social psychology using psychoanalytic ideas. Key figures in developmental psychology ranging from Jean Piaget to Lev Vygotsky engaged with Freud's work and even participated in the founding of psychoanalytic associations. These early connections are absent from most psychology textbooks, and it is as if psychoanalysis is too dangerous for psychology to consider, as if it has been 'repressed' from the discipline (Burman, 2008). Later chapters in this book describe some of those early connections in more detail, and I look at what was experienced in psychoanalysis as being so threatening to the kind of laboratory-experimental psychology that wanted to be taken seriously as a science.

As advocates of the 'paradigm revolution' pointed out, psychology itself is on very shaky ground when it claims to be 'scientific', for it has no agreed model of its object of study and it scorns detailed case studies in favour of experiments and surveys which aggregate results of observations from large numbers of subjects (Harré and Secord, 1972). The 'turn to language' which inspired a new generation of qualitative researchers conceptualized its object of study as being a reflexive 'self-monitoring' subject rather than an object pushed around like a billiard ball (knocked into action by what psychologists like to think of as being 'independent variables'), and it favoured detailed description of action and experience in different situations. In this way the new paradigm not only championed human agency but it showed that qualitative research in psychology could be more scientific than the old laboratory-experimental methods (Harré, 2004). What the 'crisis' debates shied away from was an engagement with psychoanalytic ideas which looked to unconscious forces that disrupted laboratory-experimental ambitions to forge a science based on the prediction and control of behaviour. And psychoanalysis also, of course, raises questions about human agency and about unconscious forces that cannot directly be reflexively monitored by the subject.

The 'turn to discourse' shifted attention to the organization of language independent of individual speakers and listeners (or writers and readers), and though 'discursive psychology' has wanted to treat psychoanalytic description as just a kind of psychological 'discourse' (Parker, 1992, 2002), the idea that there were symbolic phenomena that were affecting the way we thought and behaved did put psychoanalysis back on the agenda again. Despite their own intentions in wanting to give an 'objective' empirical description of language, the discourse-analytic researchers often offered interpretations of discursive or ideological processes that cried out for psychoanalytic explanation. Very soon this issue was addressed by writers who went on to develop 'psychosocial studies' as a new sub-field (Frosh *et al.*, 2001, 2003). This line of work re-energized the arguments made by those who had used post-structuralist, feminist and Marxist ideas, some of whom now enthusiastically took up psychoanalysis as an interpretative framework (Henriques *et al.*, 1984/1998; Hollway and Jefferson, 2000).

So what is so different about the psychoanalysis that is re-emerging now in psychology, and why should it not be seen as an archaic remainder of old psychological discourse? It is true that some adherents of psychoanalysis today do see it as a complete explanation, and press their data into shape to fit a psychoanalytic story. There are some who treat psychoanalysis as a worldview and evangelize about it just as avidly as do supporters of other kinds of psychological theory (Frosh and Baraitser, 2008). In that sense, psychoanalysis is indeed something that becomes just another 'psychological' theory, and so we need to be very sceptical about its truth claims. In my view, psychoanalytic discourse has become all-powerful in contemporary capitalist society not because it is 'true' but because it shapes the subjectivity of people who embrace it, and also a good number of those who loathe it but who still refer to their unconscious and puzzle about the meanings of their dreams and worry about the impact of early childhood events on their personalities (Parker, 1997).

I argue in this book for an approach to psychosocial research that is compatible with the broad discursive and social constructionist tradition, and I do think that some forms of psychoanalysis are more amenable to this approach than others (Parker, 2011b). And it is that way of bringing Freudian and post-Freudian ideas into research that makes the 'psychosocial' turn to subjectivity so different. We have an opportunity here to dismantle the constellation of power relations enforced by the 'psy-complex' – the theories and practices in the academy and in the clinic that describe and prescribe what is normal and what is abnormal – and to challenge the 'psychologization' of contemporary culture, which globalizes individualistic explanations in the popular media and everyday common-sense discourse (Ingleby, 1985; Rose, 1985, 1996; De Vos, 2012).

These are the stakes for which we play in psychosocial research, and so the question is whether the psychoanalysis we use today will reinforce the power of the psy-complex and the ideological force of psychologization – psychoanalysis as an insidious new 'truth' that we cannot shake ourselves from when psychologists bewitched by it keep telling us to speak in the peculiar language that they are using to describe us – or whether psychoanalysis opens up the contradictions in the apparatus and popular discourse of psychology and gives us space to reconfigure our subjectivity for ourselves. This book takes that second path, and it explores consequences of that path for the way we now engage with psychological theory and practice.

Psychoanalytic ideas in psychosocial studies

When we handle psychoanalytic ideas in this way, treating them carefully and taking them seriously, we are able to do justice to the complexity of human subjectivity without returning to the reduced image of the human being as a kind of 'object' in old psychology. One of the paradoxes of the laboratory-experimental tradition was that it referred to participants in research as 'subjects', and it is for that reason that some qualitative researchers today are queasy about using that term. Even old-paradigm so-called 'post-positivist' psychologists who are still carrying out experimental studies in much the same way as before the crisis remember that those 'subjects' were often not treated with respect, and so pretend that if they do not use the term any more then this will be sufficient to deal with the problem.

When critical qualitative and psychosocial researchers use the term 'subject', however, we do so by assuming the full human and philosophical weight of the term; a 'subject' is an agent of action combining awareness and forgetfulness, mindfulness and recklessness, reasoning and unacknowledged motives (Branney, 2008). Our 'subject' is contradictory, divided between consciousness and what is unconscious, trying to make sense of reality that is not always clearly represented to it, struggling to hold together competing explanations of the world (Parker, 2005).

This is just the starting point, but from that starting point a host of opportunities and dangers lay in wait. Freud's own writings (1953–1974) contain descriptions and speculations aplenty about the relation between the past and the present, and these can be mined by psychosocial researchers to think about language and experience, including the language and experience of the researcher themselves when they are confronted with difficult or painful issues. Embedded in Freud's writings, and then taken forward by other psychoanalysts developing their own particular analytical frameworks, are constellations of concepts that can then either help us think or that can close down thinking.

From within the Frankfurt School tradition in German-speaking culture, for example, psychoanalysis was used to account for the way certainty – closure around certain fixed concepts – operated to 'defend' the subject against unpleasant ideas, or against things that they felt to be unpleasant because of direct experience, child-rearing or ideological propaganda. A concept like 'projection' could then be used to explain how a subject defensively attributed desires they had repressed onto others, and then viewed other categories of human being as threatening them. This is a powerful way of making sense of what in social psychology was once called 'intergroup relations' (Billig, 1976). Hostility to others could be interpreted by the psychoanalytic researcher as being projected out, and this gives deeper understanding of the way prejudices are reinforced. There are thus consequences for the way a psychosocial researcher will understand hatred, and the development of psychoanalysis in Germany itself can then be accounted for more fully (Frosh, 2005).

From within the French tradition of psychoanalysis that includes the work of Jacques Lacan (2006) there developed a focus on language, on psychoanalysis as a 'talking cure' which had curative effects from putting that which was hitherto unthinkable into words. Within this tradition there is a shift of emphasis from biologically wired-in ages and stages of development to the way 'symbolic' processes provide the setting for how the individual thinks about themselves at the level of the 'imaginary', and for how they deal with traumatic events which hit them from outside language and experience, from the 'real' (Parker, 2011b). This tradition of research facilitates a different understanding of racism as symbolic, as discursively structured, and gives to psychosocial research new concepts which connect with anti-racist and 'post-colonial' theory (Hook, 2011).

Some quite different ideas emerged from within what has been termed the 'British tradition' of psychoanalysis (Burgoyne and Sullivan, 1997), and here we find the work of Melanie Klein (1986) and contributions of 'object relations' psychoanalysts who emphasize the impact of infantile phantasy (spelt with a 'ph' to indicate that this fantasy is unconscious) and of early childhood experience on later development. The notions of 'projective identification' (to describe the way that projection links the subject with others and draws those others into the fantasy-world of the subject) and 'countertransference' (the unconscious responses of the subject to the loving and hateful attention paid to them by others) then provides a framework for making sense of the interrelationship between an analyst and their analysands (the psychoanalytic term for patient or client) and for the interrelationship between researcher and their object of study (Hollway, 1989).

Finally, there are some other ways to make sense of the relationship between self and others in the 'ego-psychology' tradition that developed in the United States following the migration of a generation of psychoanalysts from continental Europe fleeing from fascism in the 1930s (Hartmann, 1939/1958). Ego-psychology, the basic elements for which were also elaborated by Anna Freud (1936), describes the way that the ego develops a variety of different 'defence mechanisms' to protect itself. These defence mechanisms include 'projection', but the emphasis in ego-psychology is on the capacities of the subject to reflect on relationships and build connections with others that are both realistic and loving. This current of work has been drawn upon in qualitative research and education to develop a richer knowledge of individual experience and social structures (Hunt, 1989; Britzman, 2011).

The intimate connection between the individual and the social

Each of the different traditions in psychoanalysis tackles a pressing question which is signalled in the term 'psychosocial'; that is, how to conceptualize the link between the level of the individual 'psyche' and the 'social' world which is a precondition for us to transform ourselves from biological entities into human beings, from objects into subjects. This is the question that also connects psychosocial research with one of the key elements of 'critical psychology', the element which attends to the way that the discipline routinely reduces explanation to the level of the individual and which then ends up with an 'essentialist' psychology which locks into one image of what we could be.

Critical psychology is, among other things, an attempt to problematize the place of psychological explanations in patterns of power and ideology. In this respect it is important that we remain aware of the force of psychological knowledge, of the fact that it wields authority and power, particularly within Western societies, and particularly with reference to questions of what is normal and abnormal, and in terms of the 'truth' of deep internal states of being. For this reason, a key objective of critical psychology is to contest essentializing forms of psychology. These are those types of psychology that generate internal categories of personhood that are unchanging and timeless, that come to be thought inescapable, and that hence bear a determining influence on the subject. Determining, that is, at least in as much as that person comes to understand themselves, and how they are understood by others. In social psychology, for example, these kinds of explanations cover over the contradictions between different possible competing images of the subject, and obscure the importance of the notion of 'conflict' as such (Plon, 1974).

Essentializing trends are so much of a problem for critical psychology because such categorical ways of thinking harbour racism, sexism and various other forms of prejudice. They are often the means through which certain dominant constructions of the world – or of particular groups of people – come to be reiterated, solidified, given a kind of psychological grounding, and hence a formidable kind of 'reality'. Such essentializing trends are a prime way that constructed and political notions come to be normalized, naturalized, and to be, as we have come to say, 'psychologized' (De Vos, 2012). This, in other words, is one of the primary ways in which psychology functions ideologically. Once we understand this, it becomes clear why an overwhelming priority of critical psychology lies with tackling the way psychology mirrors and hence reproduces present-day, culturally specific and historically bound assumptions about human nature, experience and behaviour (Parker, 2007a).

When human beings are conceptually separated from each other and a 'psychological' explanation is put in place of a cultural-historical explanation for how they develop a sense of themselves and others, all manner of ideological notions about the fixed biological nature of human activity are mobilized. As well as being unable to account for the power of racist ideas in contemporary culture, mainstream psychology is then unable to account for the strong influence of sexist images of the nature of men and women. Worse, mainstream psychology has tended to reinforce those sexist (and heterosexist) images by assuming that if the descriptions that psychologists give are of an underlying nature then it must be impossible to challenge or change that nature (Lieven, 1981).

Psychosocial research into the contradictory and transformative nature of human subjectivity turns 'critical' when it is also critical of psychoanalytic concepts. This book argues that the impact of psychoanalysis needs to be understood in the context of other radical movements inside and outside the discipline. I bring Marxist theory to bear on this question, and also underlying the argument is an assumption that feminist theory and activity is crucial to our activity. Feminist critique of psychological research, for example, also at the same time has had to address the way psychoanalytic notions of 'attachment' became an integral part of the equation (Mitchell, 1974; Haraway, 1989). Feminists have long argued that the image of the individual separated from others in the discipline of psychology is a rather peculiar and stereotypically masculine one, and that we need a relational account of the connection between people, and thus of the relation between the individual and the social world (Henriques *et al.*, 1984/1998). Only then will it be possible to turn again in psychology, to take another turn to give a fully social account of subjectivity, and to turn psychology into something else.

1 Psychoanalytic theory and psychology

Conditions of possibility for clinical and cultural practice

This first chapter provides a detailed review of the way different forms of psychoanalytic theory and methodology have emerged in recent years inside psychology. I look at the opportunities for critical work and also at the problems that psychoanalysis opens up for us. The key problem is that psychoanalysis, whatever its pretensions to provide a radical alternative to mainstream psychology, is in its practice at least still part of the 'psy-complex', and so it plays a powerful part in defining and regulating subjectivity.

Here I explore traditions of psychoanalysis, and pay some attention to the usual suspects that appear in psychology textbooks, such as Jung. But I am also concerned with traditions of work from within the clinical debates that will be less familiar to psychologists. These latter traditions of work are starting to appear in critical psychological research in the field of 'psychosocial' studies.

I review the important contribution that Kleinian and object-relations theory has made to methodological developments in research, but also draw attention to some of the dangers that this holds for those who are sceptical about the claims of psychoanalysis to provide a complete alternative 'psychological' approach. The danger is that it operates as a worldview which its adherents then evangelize about. I treat psychoanalysis here as a collection of forms of clinical practice and as an array of cultural representations of internal mental states and social relations. The theoretical focus is on the status of psychoanalysis as a form of knowledge (positioned alongside and in contradistinction to psychology), on the nature of knowledge in psychology (of others by practitioners and researchers), and of forms of popularized self-knowledge (including the relationship between that self-knowledge and professional claims). This opens the way to a critical engagement with psychoanalysis in different parts of the world.

What do psychoanalysis and psychology have in common? They both encompass conceptual practices that circulate around and attempt to comprehend individual subjectivity (Frosh, 1989). Psychoanalytic theory therefore immediately takes the discipline of psychology beyond a mere description of behaviour (still dominant traditions in US academic psychology). This 'individual' subjectivity is no automatic or universal function of human nature, and so we need to keep to the fore the constructionist argument that this subjectivity is something specific to a certain point in history and to particular parts of the world (Heelas and Lock, 1981). There are many different ways of characterizing this historical and geographical specificity, but it is possible to argue that this individual subjectivity flowered first with the birth of capitalism in Europe, though this claim needs to be modulated through a detailed analysis of the relationship between European capitalism and the 'rest of the world'.

Not only is this individual subject circled around and reflected upon in the manifold discourses that comprise psychoanalytic and psychological traditions of thought, constituted at a certain time and place, but the point from which we (psychologists or psychoanalysts) conduct such inquiry is simultaneously constructed; the individual subjects (experimenters, researchers, theorists) who conduct the analysis of their target individual object/subject (selves, clients, patients) are the product of particular cultural and institutional conditions. The point from which the inquiry is conducted thus has a peculiar mirror-like relationship with the object of inquiry (a relationship that provides the basis of a number of reflexive ethical questions in psychoanalysis and psychology). One response to this mutual implication of social constructions might be to conclude that the inquiry is thus 'impossible', and one of the differences between psychology and psychoanalysis then starts to appear; for psychology has traditionally insisted that the contradictions that inhere in the reflexive implication of researcher and researched can be ignored, resolved or transcended – that it can be made possible (e.g. Finlay and Gough, 2003; cf. Mather, 1997) – while psychoanalysis in its most radical forms has tended to draw the conclusion that this 'impossibility' lies at the very core of the subject (e.g. Freud, 1937; Malone, 2000).

The double construction of subject and object (whether of theoretical or empirical research) operates alongside a third aspect of construction, which is that the conceptual apparatus that we bring to bear on subjectivity itself is artifice (if not also artifice necessary to live in a world that has itself been made by human beings rather than being the product of an omniscient super-intelligent designer). Psychoanalysis and psychology are conceptual apparatuses that form subjects of which they speak, and also the kinds of subjects that speak about the objects they circle around.

The relationship between psychoanalysis and psychology is marked by differences over conceptual focus and methodological grounding, over ontological and epistemological claims. There has been a shift in the terms of debate between psychoanalytic and psychological work over the last century such that methodology and associated epistemological issues have come to assume priority over ontological questions, over the way concepts are defined and then amenable to translation from one sphere of work to the other. This shift has been driven, in part, by the development of psychology from being an enterprise primarily concerned with 'naming the mind' (Danziger, 1997) to becoming an academic and professional discipline defined almost entirely by method (Rose, 1985).

The production of genealogical and reflexive 'histories' of psychology in the last thirty years has been made possible by the emergence of a nascent tradition of 'constructionist' work that brings together once again, but now in a more complex way, conceptual and methodological aspects of inquiry (e.g. Richards, 1996; Rose, 1985). It has thus been possible to interrogate anew ontological and epistemological foundations of modern subjectivity, and thus to explore the historical nature of psychological (and psychoanalytic) theory and practice. One might say that the emergence of the alternative constructionist tradition provides the 'conditions of possibility' or, at the very least, a 'surface of emergence' for new discourses about psychology and psychoanalysis that do not take the objects of those different spheres of inquiry as given (Blackman, 1994; Foucault, 1969/1972; Hook, 2005).

To treat psychoanalytic clinical practice as a component of the broader 'psy-complex', for example, enables us to destabilize the 'truth effects' of psychoanalysis while taking seriously the production of particular forms of subjectivity (Miller and Rose, 1988, 1994). Both psychology and psychoanalysis have a peculiar power in modern society to produce what they find, and to do so within particular institutions and cultural practices such that they are able to incite, mobilize and recruit human subjects who will testify to the 'truth' of their investigative procedures and their determinate knowledge. The different spheres of inquiry are not mere theoretical frames for making sense of human experience, then, but should each be treated as a conceptual apparatus which is tied to specific modes of inquiry and self-confirmation.

At the same time the constructionist movement in modern psychology goes well beyond the 'cognitive turn' (cf. Talvitie and Tiitinen, 2006), and that movement has opened up a useful but still limited space for addressing the nature of our knowledge of subjectivity (e.g. Gergen, 1985). The relationship between the conceptual apparatuses of psychology and psychoanalysis is becoming an increasingly urgent question for adherents of each apparatus. This chapter sets out some of the coordinates for the emerging debates over the role of psychoanalytic theory and clinical practice in psychology and elaborates some ways of mapping the conditions of possibility for the emergence of psychoanalysis inside psychology, now as part of 'our' own conceptual apparatus for defining and treating modern subjectivity.

Freud and the rest

Psychology undergraduate textbooks in the English-speaking world (and then those produced by US publishers in other languages) tend to represent Freud's (1953–1974) writings as rather archaic remainders in the distant history of the discipline. Here his work is systematically mis-represented, corralled into a scientific paradigm that he questioned and then judged according to criteria he refused. Psychoanalysis thus functions as the exemplary 'unscientific' approach to understanding the individual while, at the same time, ages and stages of development are described in the same textbooks and attributed to Freud (Richards, 1989). The rhetorical motif of 'Freud/Jung/Adler' (with the series continued sometimes with a few later analysts) is then taken up by many of those who teach psychoanalytic 'personality theory' to psychology students; and although Jung and Adler broke from Freud and explicitly disowned psychoanalysis (to found their own brands of 'analytical psychology' and 'individual psychology'), and even though the different theories must all be revised by students for examination, psychoanalysis is still often treated as a compressed mass of notions ranging from 'penis envy' to the 'collective unconscious' and the 'inferiority complex'.

The case of Jung (1983) is particularly relevant to a consideration of the relationship between psychology and psychoanalysis, all the more so when questions of 'culture' are to the fore in such research. Jung not only provides theoretical resources for assessing 'personality types', but he also claims to embed these individual categories in anthropological discoveries concerning the commonalities and differences between cultures (e.g. Jung, 1989). There has even been some interest in Jung's writings among the newer traditions of 'constructionist' theory in psychology – though, as we shall see, these are most strange bedfellows. It is worth rehearsing some of the key theoretical compass points of Freudian psychoanalysis and differentiating them from this tradition, with which Freud's work is commonly confused, before turning to more recent attempts to engage with psychoanalytic theory in psychology. These questions are particularly important given the popularity of Jungian conceptions of self and culture with 'new age' therapists in the English-speaking world who are unaware of the reactionary history of Jung's writing.

Jung was the first President of the International Psychoanalytical Association (IPA), founded in 1910 by Freud and his followers in Nuremberg. Freud had proposed Jung as 'permanent president' of the IPA, but was relieved when Jung eventually resigned after three years of presidency (Gay, 1988). When Jung broke from the IPA, he made it clear that he was developing something that was quite different from psychoanalysis; but why was Freud so pleased that the differences had at last been clarified, above and beyond being delighted to be rid of 'the brutal holy Jung and his pious parrots' (Gay, 1988: 241)?

First, psychoanalysis is concerned primarily with questions of 'form' rather than of 'content'. The Oedipus complex, for example, does not prescribe roles for women and men so that each child can really be in love with mother and want to kill father. The 'father' and 'mother' are, rather, functions that may be physically embodied in the same individual care-giver or distributed among many others. What are most important are the *formal* properties of the relationship; the infant's love for its first object is broken by another figure so that the infant may be inducted into wider social relationships (Freud, 1933). Jung, on the other hand, filled out the formal structures with collective material from mythology that is imagined to be present as content to each individual; and so a Jungian learns the content of myths in order that each person can be read as if they were a pack of living tarot card characters.

Second, psychoanalysis focuses on the *disjunction* between consciousness and the unconscious; the unconscious is not conceived as being like another version of consciousness that can be accessed and so harmonized with what we are immediately aware of, and the unconscious does not contain a centre that can be detected so that real intentions can be brought to the surface. If dreams are, as Freud said, a royal road to an understanding of the unconscious, it is because dreams help us track around the boundaries of the unconscious, not because the road actually leads into it so we can see it as it is (Freud, 1900/1999). Against this, Jung relies on a number of holistic assumptions in which there is a unity of self, and potentially there is unity between consciousness and layers of the personal and collective unconscious.

Third, psychoanalysis treats every appeal to divine forces as a sign of pathology, as symptomatic, and religious ideas are usually seen as illusions or delusions that provide varying measures of comfort or security (even if some practising psychoanalysts modify this stance in order not to pathologize religious belief). The questioning and dismantling of all 'ideals' makes psychoanalysis necessarily atheist, and its clinical and political practice arose as part of the tradition of the Western Enlightenment: *reason* allied with scientific inquiry (Freud, 1930 [1929]). Jung, on the other hand, sought to 'reconnect' individuals with a domain of spiritual experience, and this is a domain which combines what he sees as essential and universal in life (Dalal, 1988).

Jung's 'analytical psychology', then, was not at all compatible with the laboratory-experimental paradigm that governed, and still predominates, in mainstream academic and professional psychology. Psychology is neither monolithic nor immutable, however, and changing relationships between various currents of work have provided some points of connection between psychology and analytical psychology. The discipline of psychology is a conceptual apparatus that has increasingly shifted from questions of ontology (a domain of inquiry in which there could be some dialogue with psychoanalytic ideas) to questions of epistemology, and so increasingly to attempts to circumscribe the conditions in which we make any claims to have discovered underlying mental processes (i.e. to methodological debates endemically hostile to psychoanalysis). The interchange between psychology and psychoanalysis closed down – and this is then the point at which it might be possible to say that psychoanalysis became the 'repressed other' of psychology (Burman, 2008) – but the increasingly mechanistic character of psychology also incited humanistic and phenomenological responses; the Jungian (non-psychoanalytic) invitation to attend to content, self and spirituality was thus congenial to some critics of mainstream psychology inside the discipline, and this is now still the setting in which some few 'constructionists' are also sympathetic to Jungian ideas (e.g. Jones, 2003; Olson, 2006).

The departure of Jung from the IPA was an opportunity for Freud to clarify psychoanalysis of a number of temptations in clinical practice. The temptations include: to decipher underlying content (and then, for example, to interpret what the ostensibly real meanings of the symbols in dreams are); to discover real selves (and then, for example, to recognize and validate this seemingly whole self as it finds its way to conscious awareness); and to wallow in mysticism (and then, for example, to provide reassurance with respect to particular ideals that the analyst also shares). However, this clarification was not sufficient to protect psychoanalysis for ever, and the existence of the IPA as an organization was certainly no guarantee that Freud's work would not also start being influenced again by the idea that we must be concerned with content, unity of the self or spirituality.

After Freud

Powerful historical forces eventually pressed the IPA into a shape that was protective of psychoanalysts but not of psychoanalysis as such; as with the operation of any defence mechanisms, protection led to distortions and then to the sedimentation of the distortions such that anything that questioned its own particular orthodoxy was viewed as a threat. Psychoanalysis was virtually destroyed in central Europe with the rise of Nazism in the 1930s, and the analysts fled (Frosh, 2005). The IPA apparatus shifted to the English-speaking world, and a particular version of psychoanalysis that was concerned with the adaptation of individuals to society developed, and complemented that painful process by which the émigré analysts had to adapt themselves to new social conditions (Jacoby, 1983).

The dominant tradition in the United States, 'ego-psychology', took literally Freud's formulation of the aims of analysis in his new introductory lectures in 1933, that 'where id was, there ego shall be'. The formulation continues: 'it is the work of culture – not unlike the draining of the Zuider Zee' (Freud, 1933: 80). Here it is possible to see individuality, adaptation and civilization closely tied together; these notions, though, are actually what we have to see as problematic in order to enable psychoanalysis to take place. In the ego-psychology tradition there was once more a conception of the unity of self, something that built upon what the practitioners saw as a conflict-free sphere of the ego (Hartmann, 1939/1958).

Even in the dissident tradition following Klein (1986), which was allowed to remain inside the IPA, it was hoped that analysis would enable the ego to become 'the captain of the soul' (Hanna Segal, as cited in Bourne *et al.*, 1987: 95). This tradition of work was predicated on the notion that the unconscious was some kind of container and that objects – 'introjected' and 'projected' – moved in and out of some separate interior space (Mitchell, 1986). While this model of the mind was quite different from Freud's conception of the unconscious, it has proved to be more acceptable to some psychologists; even though descriptions Kleinians give of the content of the mind seem at first sight too outlandish – hard-wired infant knowledge of the father's penis inside the mother that provokes envious attack, for example – there is some deeper compatibility between the underlying ontological frameworks, so that the Kleinian 'alternative' operates as a bizarre mirror image of the way early forms of quasi-empiricist investigators viewed the mind before the development of the discipline of psychology as such (Leader, 2000).

Still inside the IPA, Kleinians have been elaborating detailed specifications of the content of the mind, and in the third main strand within the IPA – which now includes object-relations, interpersonal and relational psychoanalysis – there has, again, been some rapprochement with spirituality, with practitioners declaring allegiance to a range of theological traditions, ranging from Roman Catholicism (Symington, 1990) to a form of Buddhism treated as a religious system of thought (e.g. Coltart, 2000). The relationship between Klein and Lacan (2006) has also been a preoccupation of those attempting to find ways of questioning the way an individual subject is inhabited by culture (e.g. Gülerce, 2005; Shingu, 2004).

The project of strengthening the ego went alongside the strengthening of the IPA. By 1953, measures were being taken to silence or expel those who were too far out of line, in some cases involving bitter and prolonged disputes. The separation of Lacan from the IPA, for example, was a long-drawn-out process that lasted for ten years, from 1953 to 1963 (Roudinesco, 1990).

Lacanian attention to language, and thus, it would seem, to the discursive construction of subjectivity, has then also flourished as a sub-speciality of the constructionist movement in psychology (e.g. Henriques *et al.*, 1984/1998; cf. Malone and Friedlander, 2000). This incorporation of Lacanian ideas has been particularly attractive to those who read Lacan as one of a 'post-structuralist' trio; that is, alongside Foucault and Derrida (Sarup, 1988). He could be imported to take forward the new paradigm turn to language and turn to discourse inaugurated by the so-called 'crisis' in social psychology (Parker, 1989).

The temptation here, of course, is that Foucault/Lacan/Derrida are invoked as if they comprise a necessarily radical and homogeneous gang of three that would not only displace mainstream psychology but also provide theoretical rigour to really turn the paradigm crisis into a revolution (e.g. Parker, 1992). It has not only been the old humanist psychologists who have suspected that appeals to Lacanian psychoanalysis then threaten to replace mechanistic approaches with mystification that may be worse (e.g. Billig, 1999).

Constructions

As has been noted, the most significant recent engagement with psychoanalysis by psychologists has been within the broad 'constructionist' movement. (The earliest empirical studies within the 'social representations' current, a form of work that is cognate with social constructionism though often in practice uneasily linked with the positivist tradition (Voelklein and Howarth, 2005), concerned the circulation of psychoanalysts within French culture (Moscovici, 1976/2008). There have then been some attempts to connect analysis of social representations with psychoanalysis (e.g. Kaës, 1984).) Many social constructionists have also been the most determined enemies of psychoanalytic categories, seeing them as the reintroduction of individualist mechanistic images of the person that have historically been the domain of mainstream laboratory-experimental psychology. If indeed a key part of the constructionist challenge to psychology is a refusal of metaphors of 'depth' and 'interiority', then psychoanalysis should be kept at bay. If psychoanalysis has been discussed, it is then often viewed as one of the worst and most intense forms of psychology, and should not be allowed in through the back door in ostensibly 'critical' debates.

In the US pragmatist tradition of social constructionist critique and in the UK-based genealogies of the discipline of psychology, then, psychoanalysis is treated as part of the problem rather than as part of the solution (Gergen, 1991; Rose, 1996). These critics have, with good reason, been suspicious of the attempt by some of their colleagues, writers on 'discourse' and 'rhetoric', to appear to take psychoanalysis seriously. However, the turn to psychoanalytic discourse has nevertheless been attractive to some writers, whether their sceptical starting points have been based in deconstructionist, postmodern or feminist research (e.g. Haaken, 1998; Hollway, 1989).

One of the artificial dividing lines between psychology and psychoanalysis has thus been displaced to an unstable and shifting boundary between 'discourse' and psychoanalysis. It is here that the relationships between the discursive and 'pre-discursive' realms have been addressed using psychoanalytic theories of the real and the body (e.g. Frosh, 2002; Hook, 2006). The most nuanced work serves to define this boundary by crossing it and offering commentary upon it, reflecting on the difficulty both of providing an account of the construction of psychoanalytic phenomena (an account that complements and extends accounts of the construction of psychological phenomena) and of providing a conceptualization of how an embodied subject comes to engage in the production and reproduction of a constructed social world. The temptation to turn to a full-blown alternative 'psychology' based upon psychoanalysis is most of the time resisted.

One can find here researchers who work right at the edge of the boundary, attempting to find ways of addressing that line and how we might conceptualize what lies on the other side of it. From within studies of 'rhetoric', for example, a detailed analysis of the conversational strategies that enable 'repression' to take place hover on the constructionist side of the boundary and also offer new ways of theorizing the processes of sense-making that psychoanalysts have been concerned with (e.g. Billig, 1999). From within studies of 'narrative', on the other side of the line, as it were, close attention has been paid to the nature of subjectivity, and this research draws upon clinical experience to explore how psychoanalytic notions of representation and the 'real' might be conceptualized, asking how we might need to understand how discourse operates for a subject infused with a therapeutic sense of agency and loss (e.g. Frosh, 2002).

Some forms of analysis heavily influenced by the 'consciousness-raising' imperative of second-wave feminism and the subsequent employment of psycho-dynamic notions take that exploration forward. Questioning those presuppositions about the raising of consciousness, psychoanalytic work concerning the realms of the clinic and the social has moved in a wider sweep across this boundary between psychoanalysis and constructionism, taking experience seriously but then embedding it in political context (e.g. Malone and Kelly, 2004). A corresponding move, perhaps, might be identified in the work proceeding from discursive assumptions about models of individual experience and leaping across the boundary from the constructionist side of the equation into studies of the construction of psychoanalysis in an uneasy attempt to take the psychoanalysis seriously but to treat it as a necessary complement to the production of subjectivity in discourse (e.g. Parker, 1997).

That disparate and intersecting work around the boundary between discourse and psychoanalysis then introduces a trajectory within discursive work towards studies of 'subjectivity', within which quasi-autobiographical reflections are used to ground studies of social phenomena but in which the psychoanalytic side of the boundary starts to take priority over the constructionist side (e.g. Crossley, 2004). This then has serious consequences for those attempting to use psychoanalytic ideas inside psychology as a form of critique. Instead of disturbing our taken-for-granted understanding of who we are, psychoanalytic ideas may serve to ratify prevailing images of normal and abnormal behaviour.

Pincer movement

Psychologists often experience psychoanalytic theory as an incomprehensible mass of suppositions and speculations because psychoanalysis does not appear to address questions about the individual in the same way as does psychology. The expectation that psychoanalysis should frame its own research questions in the same way as does psychology introduces a tension not only between the two conceptual apparatuses but also within psychoanalytic writing itself (Forrester, 1997). Some traditions of work in psychoanalysis have been driven recently to conform to psychological models of the individual and of investigation, as a consequence of the 'crisis in psychoanalysis' (the reduction in funding through insurance schemes combined with the onslaught by critics of psychoanalysis). The news magazine of the IPA, *International Psychoanalysis*, refers in nearly every issue in recent years to the 'crisis in psychoanalysis'.

Insurance companies demand cheaper, more efficient 'evidence-based' treatments than psychoanalysis could possibly provide. Mainstream psychoanalytic clinical practice in the United States has been badly affected, for example, and there is a measure of desperation in the appeals of psychoanalytic writing to empirical studies of child development to confirm that psychoanalytic models might still be taken seriously (e.g. Stern, 1985; cf. Cushman, 1991). In the UK there have been attempts to use functional magnetic resonance imaging studies of brain activity to warrant psychoanalytic work (e.g. Fonagy and Target, 2004). One important consequence is that psychoanalysts working in the fields of child observation and 'neuro-psychoanalysis' must agree to criteria for scientific investigation that are antithetical to psychoanalysis itself (Talvitie and Ihanus, 2005). Those psychoanalysts who have tried to make psychoanalysis jump through the supposedly scientific evidence-based hoops are now all the more poorly affected when the rules are tightened up and they are excluded (e.g. Westen *et al.*, 2004).

Once this road is travelled, psychoanalytic theorists seeking approval for their work from psychologists are faced with transforming psychoanalysis so that it will turn into a kind of psychology (Fonagy, 2000), a forced choice between psychoanalysis and psychology in which they must choose psychology in a desperate attempt to save what they can of psychoanalysis but in which they will then have to give up all of the psychoanalysis in order to satisfy their new masters. This strategy does not resolve the 'crisis' in psychoanalysis; neither does it contribute to any potentially radical and productive 'crisis', any deep questioning, inside psychology. This mistaken strategy instead operates as one arm of a pincer movement that threatens genuine psychoanalytic research inside psychology.

The other arm of the pincer movement operates inside psychology, directed at those who have attempted to find psychoanalytic alternatives as part of the broader conceptual crisis that included the turn to language, turn to discourse and emergence of social constructionist perspectives. The question addressed to those who sought to use psychoanalytic notions alongside versions of social constructionist theory in psychology has always concerned this model of the individual that is perhaps presupposed but never adequately theoretically elaborated. The question, which had already been addressed to the new paradigm and discursive researchers, was over what psychological model would be put in place of that provided by the different versions of laboratory-experimental psychology (e.g. Smith, 1994).

In some cases alternative models were offered, and in others those operating within the social constructionist movement insisted that their work should circle around the empty place that mainstream psychology was too keen to fill; the argument here is that the point of alternative research was precisely that it was continually questioning the function of any model of the individual (e.g. Brown *et al.*, 1998). Research should thus be 'non-psychological' or 'anti-psychological' (see also Squire, 1989).

The employment of psychoanalytic categories by those working in the social constructionist tradition did, then, often necessitate 'refusals' rather than 'proposals' as crucial components of critical theoretical work (e.g. Adlam *et al.*, 1977). Psychoanalytic responses to psychology have, since then, been marked by ambivalence over the way the question regarding alternative models of the individual should be answered, and whether those questions should indeed be answered at all. The trap – and this is where the second arm of the pincer movement that encloses psychoanalytic research and squeezes it into a shape that will be comprehensible to psychology comes to operate – is that some psychoanalytic writers have started to answer this question. Caving in to the question goes alongside some attempts within the qualitative research tradition to turn from the level of discourse to the level of intention, motivation and unconscious material in analysis (e.g. Hollway and Jefferson, 2000).

At the same time, qualitative researchers in psychology have come under similar pressure to specify an alternative 'psychology' that might replace the one they object to in mainstream laboratory-experimental research; apart from psychoanalysis, other traditions that have unfortunately relented and now speak the language of the very psychology they once attempted to displace include 'Interpretative Phenomenological Analysis' (e.g. Smith, 2004). This approach (which is actually most often neither interpretative, phenomenological nor analytic) thus neatly complements the quasi-positivist claims of 'grounded theory' to exhaustively code data, and this response – a model of individual 'intention' combined with a method that will access it all – then satisfies some psychologists (Parker, 2005).

Again, when a psychological model is elaborated, whether it draws upon therapeutic discourse or models of childhood and the development of defence mechanisms, the game is up. The battle between psychology and psychoanalysis has been won by psychology, and what is left of psychoanalytic conceptions of subjectivity is negligible. Some small pyrrhic victories – that bits of psychoanalytic vocabulary have been smuggled into the discipline of psychology – and even, perhaps, the illusion that psychology has been swept by a new paradigm revolution in human sciences that has seen a turn to 'affect', serve to mask, all too briefly, the way the terms of the debate will then be strictly psychological.

Clinic and culture

Studies of subjectivity – whether based in psychology as counterpoint or counterweight to psychological investigations of individual behaviour, cognition or experience, or based in other human sciences in a bid to offer a more complete account of a sociological or political topic – face a particular vexed question when such studies often draw upon psychoanalysis. This question concerns the relationship between the analysis of culture and analysis that takes place in the clinic. Psychoanalytic engagements with discourse have followed this course (e.g. Dunker, 2005), as have studies of the role of psychotherapy as part of a progressive political agenda (e.g. Hayes, 1998). There have, of course, been many attempts from within psychoanalytic practice to provide accounts of cultural issues. Freud's (1921, 1930 [1929]) work on 'mass psychology' and the unease inherent in culture (in the study rendered into English in the phrase 'civilization and its discontents') gave rise to a series of attempts to explain social and political processes by way of unconscious motivations, and such explanations then came to pervade culture so that explanations of the pathology of certain political leaders draw upon psychoanalytic categories (e.g. Immelman, 1999, 2003).

Psychoanalysis does, in this respect, provide a specific cutting terminology with which to abuse enemies that is much more effective than any other variety of psychology, and this predilection to pathologize individuals as part of its 'social' explanation should be cause for concern, a warning that psychoanalysis might end up mystifying more than it illuminates when it is brought to bear on cultural issues. Here is reason enough for those involved in psychoanalytic training organizations to question the assumption that there is something distinctive and valuable that psychoanalysts might offer to our understanding of the world. The evangelical tendencies of psychoanalysts to treat their own particular clinical framework as a 'worldview' – this, in explicit opposition to Freud's (1933) insistence that it should not be – are at least as pronounced as those of psychologists and social constructionists (e.g. Gergen, 1991). Psychologists who turn to psychoanalysis as if it really were a 'depth' psychology, designed to treat psychoanalysis as part of the armoury of a more inclusive and thorough psychological explanation for social issues, will not, of course, find cause for complaint here. Anxieties that they may have over the use of psychoanalysis will only be over the choice of political targets, not over the reduction of cultural questions to the level of the individual as such. Those psychologists who are influenced by constructionist perspectives, on the other hand, will want to find ways to manage the problematic relationship between culture and the clinic, between cultural analysis and clinical psychoanalysis.

One way of managing this relationship is to argue that psychoanalytic theory has, it is true, developed from the clinical practice of Freud and his followers, but that what we have learnt about psychoanalysis now needs to be thoroughly disconnected, uprooted from the clinic (e.g. Jacoby, 1975). Either then clinical psychoanalysis should be treated as part of the problem, something to be investigated by psychoanalytic social theory that is honed to examine cultural questions but stripped of its tendencies to reduce explanation to the level of the individual (e.g. Kovel, 1988), or the clinic should be treated as a resource for some theoretical ideas but as lying completely outside the remit of social analysis (e.g. Nasio, 1998). The political problems that attend psychoanalysis as a practice that adapts people to culture would thus be dealt with by turning it into a cultural practice. The tensions between traditions of (British-based) psychoanalytic group therapy sometimes turn on this problematic; while the (Foulkesian) tradition of 'group analysis' was historically linked with the work of Norbert Elias but then channels social theory into the clinical domain, in a conception of clinical work as 'ego training in action' (Burman and Frosh, 2005), the alternative (Bionian) tradition was historically linked with the more orthodox and individually focused approach at the Tavistock Institute, but it then extrapolates its analyses to organizations and cultures (Trist and Murray, 1990). This would then be one plausible perspective from which to examine the relationship between psychoanalysis and psychology. Once a decision has been made to leave the clinic to the side (or to interrogate it as thoroughly as one does any other treatment modality), psychoanalytic 'social theory' can position itself as a critique of all kinds of psychology and 'psychologization', the process by which academic and cultural questions are transformed into questions about the nature of individual psychology.

There is, however, another different, diametrically opposite way of addressing the problematic relationship between the psychoanalytic clinic and culture. This argument would be that psychoanalysis started, as the social theorists acknowledge, as a clinical practice, but that the concepts only operate in the space of the clinic, that a certain kind of relationship is constituted in clinical practice in which 'transference' comes to function, and then that the analysis of the unconscious is only possible within this transferential relationship. It would then, within this view, be illegitimate to conduct analyses of individuals (or of cultural phenomena) that are not constituted under transference, that are not constituted in the way an analysand speaks to the analyst. The question of the 'applied' nature of psychoanalysis here does not revolve around certain categories of subject trained to analyse others but around the structural institutional nature of the relationships within which the 'analysis' is elaborated.

There are a number of corollaries to this argument that then also, simultaneously, carry ethical implications for the practice of psychoanalysis inside and outside the clinic (Parker, 2011b). The first is that the 'clinical space' should not be treated as sacrosanct, but should be treated itself as *cultural space* in which certain institutionally structured phenomena occur, including, crucially, transference (Nasio, 1998). Second, although there is not transference as such in cultural space, the pervasiveness of psychoanalytic discourse can constitute relationships as if they are transferential, but there is then an obeisance of cultural practices to clinical practices that needs to be questioned and unravelled (e.g. Samuels, 1993a). This is related to the debate within psychoanalysis over the extent to which transference should be 'interpreted': psychoanalysts of all stripes work within the transference, but many psychoanalysts now argue that to draw attention to the transference as part of an interpretation often amounts to little more than suggestion (Cottet, 1993). In addition, at the end of analysis, the analyst might expect that such a transferential effect will be transformed, even to the point where interpretation as such is no longer of any use.

Conclusions

Psychoanalysis started with the attempt to conceptualize and treat hysteria (Breuer and Freud, 1895). The map of the body that enables the subject to produce physical symptoms does not correspond to organic muscle groups, and it is therefore clear that there is a psychic cause to the particular pain or paralysis in question (the symptom, personal history and life-world of the subject is, we might say, 'constructed'). Maps of the world are just as revealing of underlying symptomatic assumption and problems in dealing with history.

Derrida once pointed out that the constitution of the International Psychoanalytic Association which was ratified at the thirtieth Congress in Jerusalem defines the three main geographical areas of the IPA's world: 'America north of the United States – Mexican border; all America south of that border; and the rest of the world' (1998: 75). Derrida (who was born in Algeria, trained in France and taught in the United States) then proceeded to a close reading of the constitution and its notion of 'human rights' to raise questions about the naming of Latin America and the ethical practices that psychoanalysts have been confronting in that part of the world, and of naming 'torture' as a particular problem that some analysts have been implicated in.

The 'map' that an organization representing psychoanalysts employs to understand its place in the world and its relation with history thus provides some warnings and lessons for constructionist-oriented psychologists seeking to understand the relationship between different conceptual apparatuses. The current listing of 'IPA Constituent Organizations' rectifies this problem, to an extent. Still, there are again three main geographical areas: 'Europe, including Australia, India and Israel', 'Latin America' and 'North America including Japan' (IPA, 2006).

If we step back and look at the development of psychoanalysis around the world we can see how provincial this representation of the approach is. In

Japan, for example, every form of psychoanalysis that Western psychologists would recognize, and more, coexist with quite different representations of subjectivity that are also strangely psychoanalytic (Parker, 2008). Our critiques of mainstream psychology also need to include acknowledgement that we should develop a critique of psychoanalysis as such and, just as with a critique of psychology, the resources to undertake this critique already exist in the 'rest of the world', wherever that rest of the world is for us where we are in our little bit of it (Dafermos *et al.*, 2006, 2013).

2 Psychoanalysis and critical psychology

This chapter connects the issues we have explored in the last chapter with the domain of critical psychology. The chapter provides a systematic exploration of the way that different forms of psychoanalysis can be used as a resource by critical psychologists, but I also look at some of the dangers of importing theories that pretend to give a universal account of psychology to combat mainstream psychological ideas. You will see here many examples of how we may be jumping out of the frying pan of psychology into the fire of psychoanalysis, and how that supposedly 'alternative' psychoanalysis is itself often just another form of the psychology that we wanted to escape.

The material is from a chapter in a book on critical psychology which was published in South Africa in 2004, and so here I take forward the point I made in the previous chapter about the importance of learning about different debates in psychology and psychoanalysis around the world. South Africa has been a particularly powerful testing ground for psychological theories, and has showed most psychological and psychoanalytic theories to be wanting when it comes to the general question of sensitivity to cultural context and to the specific question of racism.

We are able to see that we have to give up the idea that new psychoanalysis can offer us a tried and tested alternative to old-paradigm psychology, which itself is structured by the history of racism in Europe. Psychoanalysis also poses questions for other theoretical resources that we might use. Some alliances can be made, and as well as alliances there are some points of serious dispute with other approaches within critical psychology, and some warnings for those wanting to develop 'psychosocial' alternatives based on psychoanalytic ideas.

One of the oldest modes of psychological explanation is that of psychoanalysis. Psychoanalysis in its dominant English-speaking forms, for example, has long tried to interest psychologists in its work and it has sought to legitimate itself by drawing on mainstream psychological research. Clearly, psychoanalysis does not necessarily lead us to be critical, and it does not necessarily oppose the essentializing trends of much psychology; at times it even extends them. Hence one of the principal objectives of this chapter is to take to task a number of psychoanalytic explanations – principally those of Kleinian psychoanalysis – that work in the essentializing ways described above. The second objective of this chapter also lies with a critical scrutiny of psychoanalysis. Here, however, the objective is to bring to the surface those radical elements of psychoanalytic theory that are generally 'screened out' by the ideological concerns that have come to structure psychology. It seems that there is some radical potential within psychoanalysis, a potential that we should not reject out of hand just because certain applications of psychoanalysis have been politically conservative. Here it is just as important to consider those kinds of psychoanalysis that have *not* been put to popular use, as those that have. If it is the case that psychology is structured around the ideological preoccupations of capitalist society, that it constructs what it pretends to discover – namely (and mostly typically) the alienated competitive subject of capitalist society – then any articulation of subjectivity that would extend beyond this framework would be systematically filtered out (Parker, 1997). It most certainly does seem to be the case that a great deal of psychoanalytic theory has been 'ideologically domesticated', brought into line with a series of status quo assumptions and understandings of the day. This, however, is not all that psychoanalysis has to offer. Such ideologically domesticated uses of psychoanalysis do not exhaust all of its potential critical extensions or application (Hook, 2011).

Psychoanalysis as against essentialist psychology

Psychoanalysis precisely poses a question to us about who we are and how we have come to be, a question that is necessarily one without a clear answer, one that defies any attempt to find underlying essential psychological processes. What we need to document, as part of our critical attention to the ideological forms that are very compatible with mainstream psychology, and to avoid, in the development of our own perspectives, are those reactionary motifs which tell us that *we cannot change society because we cannot change the underlying nature of human beings.* Here we see a form of psychological thinking which is very powerfully ideological – it discourages any attempt to change society, and makes our current circumstances appear as if they are the *only way they ever could have been*, as if there are no real social, political, historical alternatives. Some of these most reactionary motifs appear when psychoanalysis makes racial difference into an essential asymmetric difference that is impossible to change.

We will now turn to look at how different varieties of psychoanalysis might be helpful or otherwise to the project of critical psychology. I will do this, first, by looking at how psychoanalytic approaches serve to *essentialize* their accounts in the name of truth (that is, to find fixed things under the surface that will explain everything). Second, I will draw attention to how psychoanalysis might work *pragmatically* in the service of critical work (that is, how it might be tactical and open to different possibilities that might be useful to us). Third, I will open a space for reflection on the *construction* of psychoanalysis's own accounts (to look at how its arguments have been formed in distinct cultural contexts). In each case we will look at institutional processes, clinical work and research strategies. The question here is how to understand the way psychoanalysis takes root in a culture, how it might function to relieve distress and how we might make psychoanalytic ideas useful for critical research in psychology.

Essentialist psychoanalysis: opportunities and dangers

One of the problems with psychoanalysis is that people who really believe it try to spread it with an evangelistic zeal that makes every phenomenon that it studies fit into a grid of *hidden fixed essences*. There is an essentialism in much English-speaking psychoanalysis that becomes evident in the attempts to bring the good word once again to Africa in training institutions modelled on those in Western Europe. We find this essentialism also in the attempts to explain the history and effects of oppression in psychologically reductionist terms, and in the attempts to discover in research material the underlying processes psychoanalysis *knows* must be there. Here psychoanalysis works like a metanarrative; that is, a privileged form of explanation, an account, a story or a theoretical system, which is treated as superior to all others in its explanatory abilities. Psychoanalysis thus becomes the most 'real' form of explanation available, and theoretical postulates and constructs of which it speaks come to be reified. Psychoanalytic forms of explanation hence come to be projected onto the world, onto all kinds of social phenomena, with an unquestionable reality and importance. Here we see one of the central dangers of psychoanalytic thought: what had claimed to be a mode of *interpreting* the world comes instead to be a way of *constructing* it, of imposing its categories and understandings on it. Let us take the case of 'British tradition' psychoanalysis to illustrate these issues.

British psychoanalysis has been heavily influenced by the work of Melanie Klein, and one of the three factions in the British Psychoanalytical Society consists of followers of her ideas. Kleinian psychoanalysis is a good example of 'essentialist psychoanalysis'. For Kleinians the unconscious is conceptualized as being like a separate space in the mind outside conscious awareness that is full of different 'instincts' which have direct representation in objects. The mind is assumed to be heterosexual, and this basic characteristic is seen as biologically wired in; the infant already unconsciously knows, for example, what the difference between men and women is. The infant (and adult) defends themself from these unconscious instinctual forces by using mechanisms like 'projective identification', in which they expel unpleasant objects from their own minds into the minds of others. Kleinians are concerned with relations between 'objects', then, but they differ from 'object-relations' theory in psychoanalysis because Klein sees the defensive processes as happening inside the mind of the individual rather than between people. The most extreme defences of 'splitting' into good and bad objects occur during the 'paranoid-schizoid' position, and Kleinians claim that there is a developmental shift in the infant from the paranoid-schizoid position (characterized by acute fear and hostility and defended by splitting into the good and the bad) to the 'depressive' position in which we recognize that we have ambivalent feelings towards other people. Not only is Klein's view of the mind very grim, but she sees these destructive and defensive processes as universal and unchanging. For Kleinians these are 'developmental' processes, but they also assume that we flip from one 'position' to the other throughout adult life, and so psychoanalysis in this tradition aims to bring the patient from a paranoid-schizoid position to a depressive position.

Now we can take each of the components of the problems in essentialist psychoanalysis in turn, looking at institutional, clinical and research aspects of this approach.

Institutional contexts for new forms of colonialism

Psychoanalysis has a built-in fail-safe mechanism that kicks in when critical researchers try to use its ideas and then want to reflect on its limitations. We can see this mechanism as a 'defence mechanism' that manifests itself in the argument that only those who have been through analysis themselves can understand what psychoanalysis is, and so only practising psychoanalysts are in a position to comment on the shortcomings of the approach. (The idea of 'defence mechanisms' refers to the strategies that we are thought to use to protect ourselves from psychic pain, or from thoughts and memories that evoke pain.) A defence mechanism is something that psychoanalysis typically detects *in individuals*, but psychoanalytic theory becomes politically useful when we can use it not simply to analyse individuals, but, perhaps more importantly, to *analyse institutions*. It is in this sense that psychoanalysis can operate institutionally as a self-protecting discourse. This argument needs to be tackled by critical psychologists, who are not even engaged in clinical work, because it has a number of serious implications for any kind of radical work. The consequences of this traditional psychoanalytic argument also draw attention to the need for careful scrutiny of psychoanalysis by critical psychologists.

Institutionalized psychoanalysis in South Africa

One consequence of the way that institutional psychoanalysis discredits unqualified psychoanalytic accounts is that countries such as South Africa that do not have local training organizations controlled by the International Psychoanalytical Association (IPA) end up having their own indigenous 'psychoanalytic' work discredited. (The International Psychoanalytical Association is the organization set up by Freud and the one that dominates discussions of psychoanalysis in the English-speaking world.) Those psychoanalysts who have been trained outside the country are then in an extraordinarily privileged position to comment on the worth of local psychoanalytic research. It would, of course, be bad enough if there were local IPA trainings, because this would still mean that only certain people would have the right to speak with authority about psychoanalysis. But with the end of apartheid, there is now an even greater risk of colonization by those operating *outside* the country. The British Psychoanalytical Society, for example, includes a very large, mainly white South African émigré membership, and there are now concerted attempts for this local IPA in Britain group to move into the new South Africa and make sure that trainings operate according to its own criteria. Organizations linked to the IPA in Britain, such as the Tavistock Institute, have also been busy trying to set up local trainings. One task of critical psychologists is to argue that psychoanalysis is a diverse practice, and that it should not be defined by *any one tradition* in any particular organization. What we are becoming aware of within psychoanalytic discourse, then, is a very hierarchical approach to truth, a tendency to disqualify opposing interpretations or explanations, a tendency *to control the way psychoanalysis is used to explain*. It is small wonder then that radical forms of psychoanalytic theory have been *under-represented* in the wealth of psychoanalytic discourse that circulates in contemporary culture. Of course, this attempt to control psychoanalytic discourse is not only a question of regulating psychoanalysis as a form of knowledge and explanation; it has implications for the structure of the organization, and for how it categorizes and understands people, and its members. Indeed, there is at the moment a particular danger for gay men and lesbians, for the IPA trainings still treat heterosexuality as 'normal', and so there is a risk of importing some deeply reactionary ideas about the construction of sexuality (Kottler, 1997).

Clinical explications of political history

When we turn to the clinical implications, we find some interesting suggestions in psychoanalysis as to how identity is constructed. The danger here, however, is that the authority of the argument is assumed to lie with psychoanalysis *as a universal truth.* Some of the best critical work on racism, for example, slides from specific descriptions of present-day racism into a message about what unchangeable human nature *is really like.* When Melanie Klein (1986) writes about aggressive phantasies of tearing, biting and the scooping out of the insides of the mother, for example, we have to ask how it is that she could note such things at a certain moment, rather than reading these descriptions as 'intrinsic to human nature' (Young, 1993: 10). Kleinian accounts are very sharp (so to speak), but it does not mean that 'the forces involved are very primitive' (ibid.). If one assumes that racism is a result of the operation of Kleinian 'primitive' defence mechanisms of projective identification, for example, the most one could hope for in clinical practice with racists or those who are the victims of racism would be a shift from a point of violent destructive pathology into a position of 'depressive' acknowledgement and forms of 'reparation' which still assume that those tendencies will always lie under the surface ready to erupt again. In other words, the use of psychoanalysis in this way comes to view racism – or other social ills – as, in an odd way, somehow 'natural', as deeply internally motivated phenomena, as intrinsic, unchanging and, worse yet, *unchangeable.* This may not have been the intention of the original theorists, but – and here lies a very important lesson for critical psychology – we need always to ask *how* a given psychological theory may be used, *what* it may be used to justify . . .

There has been a great deal of critical interest in Frantz Fanon's (1986) insights into processes of racist colonial objectification, insights which focus on the experience and identities of those subjected to racism, and which have implications for psychoanalytic accounts (e.g. Manganyi, 1973). Once again, the attempt to combine Fanon's ideas with British 'object-relations' psychoanalytic theory has certain implications for clinical work. One sympathetic response to Fanon's descriptions of the way the colonized subject attempts to integrate the denigrated image of themselves puts it this way:

> If read in an object-relations frame it is a moving account of work towards a depressive position: the black self has to be accepted, first in jubilant relief that this is possible, then slowly the damage done to it in the course of its previous denigration by the subject acknowledged and mourned.
>
> (Davids, 1996: 232)

Again, the 'depressive position' is something that could be sabotaged at any moment by paranoid-schizoid splitting. Again, a clinical interpretation of a political phenomenon risks universalizing what it is speaking about, 'naturalizing' it, making it inescapable, and putting its own terms of explication before the terms of more considered historically, socially and politically specific types of explanation (Hook, 2011).

Research in which you've been framed

There is a problem when psychoanalysis is treated uncritically, as if it really did know about internal mental processes that can be uncovered in the course of research. Critical psychologists should be wary whenever they read a text which starts to tell them what the mind of the infant is really like, for at these points we are buying into implications not only for clinical treatment but also for the ethics of research. Some recent qualitative research on fear of crime in Britain, for example, uses Kleinian theory to interpret interview material. Once again, there is a risk of sliding from an illuminating account of the way fear of crime *can* be understood, into an assumption *that the description is the explanation!* We can see how this occurs in an approach which sees fear of crime as 'consistent with a paranoid-schizoid splitting of good and bad' (Hollway and Jefferson, 2000: 20). Here, once the description is treated as true, everyone is made to fit into psychoanalytic categories: 'different people will be characterized by a predominance of one or the other defensive organization – the paranoid-schizoid and depressive – as their typical response' (Hollway and Jefferson, 2000: 21). The use of psychoanalytic explanation here seems far more concerned with itself, with further extending and 'verifying' its own concepts and categories, than in being adapted to explain the world we are able to witness.

There are also implications for the ethics of research in this hard-line Kleinian tradition which directly contradict the attempts by critical psychologists to make the process of research into one which is open to participants as 'co-researchers'. This approach also makes it difficult to do anything corresponding to 'action research'; that is, those forms of research where researcher and research subjects, or, more accurately, *research participants*, work together to produce research and to bring about certain forms of social or political change. If one treats the interview material as if it were clinical material that can be subjected to psychoanalytic interpretation, then it is understandable that the researcher would not want to negotiate their accounts with their participants. Hollway and Jefferson (2000: 100), for example, are happy to talk about the 'honesty' with which they approached 'the data openly and even-handedly', but because of the nature of the interpretations they are making they cannot be honest with their participants, and they say that they do not take their interpretations back for feedback for 'ethical' reasons. Here there is a perfectly logical argument, but only if one works on the premise that critical research should be based on the model of Kleinian clinical practice. Psychoanalytic ideas that could be useful tactically, then, are turned into a form of truth that, like many other forms of mainstream psychology, protects the researcher rather than those they study. These forms of truth, moreover, are not made available to the scrutiny of those studied; they become protected 'truths' – another instance of psychoanalytic discourse being used in a selective, qualified way, in which certain people can make proclamations about the world that others cannot question.

For critical psychologists, things so far do not look so good for psychoanalysis, even if the approach throws up some intriguing suggestions as to how we might think about politics, therapy and research. A typical 'critical psychological' move here might be to deconstruct the claims to truth of psychoanalysis, to treat these claims to truth as if they themselves were structured by 'projective identification'. In each case we see an attempt to force material on another and to get them to accept it as the truth. While this would be an intriguing exercise, because it would subject psychoanalysts to their own favourite procedures, we do not really need psychoanalysis to make sense of this process. An attention to history and power will do fine, as it does in all critical psychology worth the name. But let us turn to some ways that psychoanalysis might sit more easily alongside critical work in and against the discipline.

Pragmatic psychoanalysis: questioning subjectivity and history

Despite what was said at the beginning of this chapter about the dangers of essentialism, it is possible to work with a 'strategic essentialism', precisely to take seriously how forms of identity have been historically linked with certain forms of oppression. The strategy here is to speak from a position (of being a woman, of being black, for example) because that is the way one is already positioned by others. It is a 'strategy' because it refuses to take for granted the categories used by others, and it plays with those categories in order to free the subject from those categories as fixed. Strategic essentialism enables us to grasp how we have been made into subjects structured by notions of sex and race (for example) that are woven into patterns of power. Likewise, strategic essentialism helps us to grasp how those who have been denied the right to speak may now exercise that right, precisely in order to dismantle those oppressive structures. The development of US psychoanalysis is a case in point, which shows us how assumptions about the value of identity actually run counter to the critical questioning ethos of psychoanalytic work today.

United States psychoanalysis developed its own culturally specific images of individual psychology after the Second World War, and its main aim was to ensure the healthy functioning of the individual in society. This is why it is a good example of a 'pragmatic' way of approaching problems and trying to fix them in psychoanalysis. For US psychoanalysis the unconscious is seen as a part of the mind that needs to be integrated into consciousness, and psychoanalysts working in this tradition assume that there is a 'conflict-free' part of the mind – the ego – which develops as the rational problem-solving part of the mind that it is the task of psychoanalysis to develop further. Unconscious sexual desires are seen as sometimes disruptive, but the idea is that if they can be channelled into healthy wholesome activities then they should not then be felt to be a problem. The 'ego' is also the site of reflexive awareness of who we are and what our relationships are with others. The US vision of the individual is therefore quite optimistic, closer to humanist psychology, and the 'development' of the individual and of civilization are seen as progressive linear processes which should go hand in hand together. The developmental model applied to parts of the world which are supposedly emerging from a less 'civilized' state and the idea that individuals should adapt themselves to society in order to behave in a civilized and healthy way are 'pragmatic' then, but of course they are 'pragmatic' seen from a US point of view.

The questioning of how the subjectivities of the oppressors and oppressed have been historically constituted is a more pragmatic use of psychoanalysis. Let us turn to institutional, clinical and research aspects of this pragmatic approach.

Institutional struggle to reclaim history from psychology

Psychoanalysis is woven into history, and a crucial part of the project of critical research in psychology is to show how psychoanalytic ideas have been buried. The discipline of psychology rests on psychoanalysis, though the long-standing connection between psychologists and psychoanalysts is often obscured. There is also a hidden history of psychoanalysis in South Africa that speaks to the attempt to make sense of the different positions of cultural groups. One example of such a hidden history of psychoanalysis in South Africa is to be found in Wulf Sachs's (1996) *Black Hamlet*, which is a case study of Sach's psychoanalysis of a young black man, John Chavafambira. Chavafambira was a diviner-healer in Zimbabwe, a *nganga*, before coming to South Africa to work in hotels and restaurants in Durban and Johannesburg.

Black Hamlet (first published in 1937, although followed by a revised edition ten years later entitled *Black Anger*) presents an account of everyday racism in South Africa. The book explores the deep and eventually politicizing effects on John Chavafambira, and also the effects on the relationship between black indigenous healing and white psychoanalysis (Sodi, 1999). Perhaps it was because Wulf Sachs was a little more sensitive than many other psychoanalysts of the time to the life difficulties of John Chavafambira that he was able to work with the specific questions that his patient raised. Sachs did at least try to understand that, because his patient came from a culture different to himself, it would be necessary to work differently. One should also note here that Sachs did not use his psychoanalytic encounters with Chavafambira as a basis to posit essentialist categorical differences between black and white, as much social science research of the time did (Bertoldi, 1998).

Nonetheless, Sachs's case study raises questions for critical psychologists, such as a concern with how his interpretation is already 'cued in' by the title. Clearly, *Hamlet* is already a story from Europe about a man's relationship with his dead father and his rivalry with another figure who has stepped in to take the father's place regarding the affections of his mother. We need ask here whether even a well-intentioned form of psychoanalytic interpretation might be seen to be reading a European cultural narrative into the African context.

We should also note that the story of John Chavafambira is also embedded here in a history of psychoanalysis as a peculiar kind of 'indigenous' healing practice which was brought by Jewish immigrants to South Africa but which itself was subject to some serious repression during the years of apartheid. The practice of psychoanalysis itself, in other words, often taken to be a 'Jewish science' scorned and suppressed by anti-Semitic and apartheid forces alike, was also subject to certain forms of social repression. If we look to *Black Hamlet* as a kind of historical document then, as Hayes (2002) has done, we can see how the history of psychoanalysis in South Africa, is also necessarily a history of racism.

Clinical challenges to psychoanalytic imperialism

Frantz Fanon's (1967) denunciation of colonialism and racism in *The Wretched of the Earth* has been the inspiration for revolutionaries in Africa, but it is his *Black Skin, White Masks* (1986), written shortly after he qualified as a psychiatrist, that tackles the question of racism, subjectivity and the role of psychoanalysis. The psychoanalytic context for this work was the attempt by the French psychoanalyst Octave Mannoni (1990) in *Prospero and Caliban* to explain, as the subtitle of his book put it, 'the psychology of colonization'. Mannoni drew on his experiences working in Madagascar to elaborate his understanding of the 'inferiority complex' that is suffered by the colonizers, who play the part of 'Prospero' in his account, and the 'dependency complex' that afflicts the colonized – 'Caliban' – side of the equation. As with the Kleinian accounts of racism, the descriptions of the racist mentality as characterized by 'grave lack of sociability combined with a pathological urge to dominate' (Mannoni, 1990: 102) is suitably pathologizing, and perhaps we are happy to go along with that, but the descriptions of the colonized are more problematic.

For example, Mannoni claimed that the Malagasy wanted to avoid a sense of abandonment by the white man, and although they were 'neither inferior nor superior', they were 'wholly dependent' (Mannoni, 1990: 157). This diagnosis, of course, leads to certain clinical formulations in which the treatment would focus on trying to address the sense of 'abandonment' and bring about a state of healthy 'independence'. Fanon quite rightly objected to this psychologization of colonialism, and to the implication that the fantasies of rebellion and revenge on the part of the colonized could be interpreted in terms of a 'dependency complex'.

In Mannoni we see one of the worst examples of how psychoanalytic theorizing can be used to legitimate and naturalize a kind of oppressive politics. Mannoni's suggestion is that only certain groups/races/nations can be colonized, and only certain others can be colonized, because of deep psychical processes characteristic to each of these groupings (i.e. the 'inferiority complex' that drives colonizers to colonize, and the 'dependency complex' that makes the colonized accept colonial conditions). Mannoni's theory suggests that the 'dependency complex' of the Malagasy would mean that they would experience great amounts of anxiety by the threat to established society, therefore all impulse to change a given social order would come to be avoided at all costs. Here we have a kind of emotional development destined to dependence. We are not then just talking about a distinction between 'civilized' and 'non-civilized' cultures – although with Mannoni we are certainly talking about that as well – we are dealing with the claim that certain societies have a severely hampered capacity to develop or change at all! Malagasy culture, for Mannoni (1990), is essentially static, and does not possess the potential for progress, advancement, self-betterment.

Quite aside from the moral implications of these claims – i.e. that a culture is so anxiety-prone that it fears any change and therefore is unable to muster any forms of social progress or advancement – we see here a powerful psychological validation for a massive form of sociopolitical inequality. Mannoni (1990) is effectively telling us that the basic emotional need of the Malagasy – the means through which the world is made orderly and safe – is met through establishing a bond of dependence, or more to the point, *a relationship of subordination.* If there was ever a retrograde psychoanalytic theory then this is it. Not only is Malagasy culture analysed as somehow less, as wanting, but it is considered as needing some or other form of domination, of external authority. Not only does the victim get blamed here, they are also psychoanalysed as in fact having unconsciously desired their own domination, having, worse yet, *needed* it at the cost of not being able to progress socially, culturally or technologically. Furthermore, should this relationship of dependence *not* be established, social crisis would erupt – hostility and violence would emerge from the lack of a higher patron, from the inability to establish a bond, a relationship of subordination.

Clearly then, we may suggest that political forms of analysis need at times to take precedence over purely psychical, or psychological forms of analysis. Why is this so important? It is important because otherwise psychological and psychoanalytic theories run the risk of simply reproducing the given ideological status quo. Indeed, rather than providing us with anything like a critical perspective, Mannoni's theory makes colonization sound inevitable, and, in a way, justifiable. His interpretation seems to begin with an acceptance of the framework constituted by the colonial condition, and to then 'read off' the psychology of the colonizer/colonized encounter on this basis. As such we have the case of a theory which amplifies social injustice, and reiterates the violent inequality of the colonial encounter, even while trying to explain it. Mannoni's account is, though, in a very odd sort of way, useful to us. It enables us to discern the logic of a certain kind of racism in theory which holds the oppressed responsible for their own oppression, and which derogates not on the basis of race per se, but rather on the basis of culture, notions of civilization, and progression. In this way we might suggest that the value of Fanon's *Black Skin, White Masks* lies less in the insights it gives into the psychology of those oppressed by racist colonialism, and more in the question it poses to those – like Mannoni himself – who enjoy privilege in the old colonial centres.

Research strategies that include subjectivity

One of the useful things about psychoanalysis is that it raises questions about the subjectivity of the researcher, and it helps us to reflect on our own place in any kind of research. One of the problems of mainstream psychology is that it tries to attain an objective position through an exclusion of the subjective component. Why someone should choose to research a particular topic and the way their own personal and political motives impact on the research is usually carefully screened out. Because psychoanalysis treats objectivity itself as infused with desire and fantasy, any research activity has to be subjected to reflexive inquiry. In this respect, Hunt (1989) brings to the fore a number of issues in sociological fieldwork that are relevant for critical psychologists engaged in research involving other people. She points out that a 'psychoanalytic perspective makes three assumptions foreign to most sociologists' (Hunt, 1989: 25). First, 'it assumes that much thought and activity takes place outside of conscious awareness' (ibid.). A reflexive analysis, then, is a place for exploring assumptions that we may have taken for granted, and a research team or co-supervision may be a good opportunity for turning around and looking critically at even the most 'critical' research. The second assumption is that unconscious meanings are linked to 'webs of significance which can ultimately be traced to childhood experiences' (Hunt, 1989: 25). What Hunt has in mind here is the way transference relationships with others in the course of research will replay patterns of relationships with others in childhood. The third assumption, according to Hunt, is that the psyche is 'divided into a tripartite system composed of the id, ego and superego' (1989: 25).

Now, with respect to the second and third assumptions that Hunt (1989) outlines, we have to take care once again not to buy into a whole package deal about what the structure of the mind is really like. Hunt is working in one of the dominant psychoanalytic traditions in the English-speaking world, particularly influential in the United States, that of 'ego-psychology', and so the way she describes the mind – with the ego in the middle subject to irrational forces that make it misperceive others in patterns of transference – reflects that tradition. As we saw earlier, a Kleinian view of the mind organized around 'projective identification' would see things differently. Nevertheless, Hunt does usefully draw attention to the role of subjectivity in research, and there is a connection here with some of the recent innovative work in psychology on the intersection between subjectivity, gender and race (Mama, 1995). As Mama's (1995) research makes clear, there is a feminist way of making the argument about reflexivity which draws on psychoanalytic ideas but also makes us reflect on the role of psychoanalysis as something that we may only want to use strategically in our research, as provisional and subject to question.

These strategic uses of psychoanalysis, which employ some psychoanalytic ideas while keeping the approach at a safe distance, would be viewed by psychoanalysts as indicating an underlying 'ambivalence' in the way it is being viewed, for it seems that there is something in it that is fascinating but still dangerous. In each of these three domains it is possible to be 'strategic' about what we take to be 'essential' at any moment only if we adopt a certain notion of rationality in which the ego is firmly in charge. That is, we can subject these approaches to a critical psychological reading that reveals how they rest on assumptions of ego-psychology, in which the ego is the master of the house and its task is to keep watch on forces that might disturb things. But if we reflect on the ease with which this notion of 'ambivalence' can be wheeled out to diagnose us, how psychoanalytic language is used, we are led to conceive of psychoanalysis in another way, as part of a culturally specific discourse.

Cultural psychoanalysis: working inside and alongside its discourse

Perhaps we have to take psychoanalysis seriously because it has become true for many subjects, and as they speak about things deep within they make themselves into the kind of subjects for whom psychoanalysis will work. Some of the tools from psychoanalysis for thinking about ideology might really presuppose that psychoanalysis is true, but at the same time these tools allow us to reflect on how psychoanalysis itself calls out to us so that we must recognize ourselves within it, and then it might even work as a therapeutic approach. Here we can turn to developments in French psychoanalysis to illustrate different possible paths to a form of analysis that connects subjectivity with language and culture.

French psychoanalysis has been the site for some radical re-readings of Freud's work, particularly in the tradition of the school of psychoanalysis developed by Lacan after 1964. This Lacanian tradition is a good example of how psychoanalysis might link with cultural issues, for good or ill. The Lacanian vision of the unconscious is of the 'gaps' in language, of the things that cannot be said by someone when they speak, and each individual has their own peculiar 'gaps' in speech because of their own peculiar history. Sexual desire, for the Lacanians, is always 'desire of the Other', intimately linked to what the other wants or what we perceive as being lacking in them. Lacanians do not talk about 'instincts' but of 'drives' that are discursively constructed at the very same moments that the individual constructs themself in relation to others. The image of self, or 'ego', is laid down during the mirror stage at about eighteen months old, and this image then carries on misleading us as to where the real stuff of human psychology lies. The unconscious and sexual desire are both in some sense 'outside' us, and the psychoanalyst has in some way to be 'outside' culture in order to analyse how it works. The cryptic, difficult, esoteric nature of Lacanian discourse is itself a necessary part of the endeavour to try to analyse from 'outside' everyday taken-for-granted assumptions in a culture (Parker, 2011b).

The study of language, and the language of psychoanalysis, is now one of the powerful ways of approaching psychology in a critical way, and once again we will look at institutional, clinical and research aspects.

Institutional processes structured like a language

Psychoanalytic accounts of language, which draw on the work of Lacan (1964/1973, 2006), have been very useful in showing us how ideology works to call us into a certain position, to pull us into line. In particular, the work of Louis Althusser (1971) on 'interpellation', which describes the process by which someone responds to being 'hailed' or called into position by ideology, describes how identity is constructed, reproduced and reinforced each time we respond (Hayes, 1989). Althusser likens the process of interpellation to a policeman who calls out 'hey, you there', and our immediate sense that the call is meant for us, as the guilty or good citizen. The interpellation of black citizens of the new South Africa in the frame of *ubuntu* can serve, for example, to confirm the essential identity of a community when it is sent back as a message to the community about how they should work hard and not contradict power structures. When it is used in this way, it ties the community to certain managerial and economic agendas. There are also deep implications for how the interpellation of the good citizen may be tied to certain ideas of what a good 'family' is (Hayes, 1989).

This description also has implications for how we understand the work of psychoanalysis itself. We can combine this description of interpellation into ideology with another notion from Lacan that is elaborated in greater detail by Jacques-Alain Miller, that of 'extimacy' (something that feels 'inside' us which is also in some sense 'outside'). For Miller (1986: 77), 'the extimacy of the subject is the Other', and interpellation works so powerfully because it is a process that works as if it were *inside* the subject when it is really *outside* in the organization of language. The phenomenon of being 'outside' thus marks the enduring quality of human experience that psychoanalysis brings us face to face with. There are implications here for the role of psychoanalysis in culture. Miller comments that perhaps 'it is this position of the psychoanalyst's extimacy that makes so distinct and constant the role of the Jew in the history of psychoanalysis' (Miller, 1986: 77). What Miller draws attention to here is the importance of Jews to the development of psychoanalysis – Freud and many of his followers in the psychoanalytic movement were Jewish – and the way that perhaps psychoanalysis was able to develop simultaneously as something 'inside' Western culture and as something 'outside' and critical of it precisely because of the condition of

Jews as an important part of the culture but a part that was also marginalized (Frosh, 2005). Once again, we are brought face to face with the cultural-historical nature of all theories concerning psychology.

Clinical strategies for learning analysis

What this way of thinking of psychoanalysis draws attention to is that psychoanalysis itself has to be learnt and believed in order for it to work. That 'learning' may not be explicit, for it may be absorbed through ways of speaking that we then take for granted, and then we will be 'interpellated' into the position of being a subject with an unconscious and defence mechanisms. What is 'extimate' to us will then be experienced as something deep inside us that can be accessed only by psychoanalysis.

That what is most intimate to us is really 'outside' also makes our sexual enjoyment, that which is termed by Lacan as *jouissance*, so susceptible to being 'stolen' by the Other; 'Racism is founded on what one imagines about the Other's *jouissance*; it is hatred of the particular way, of the Other's own way, of experiencing *jouissance*' (Miller, 1986: 79). This critical take on the clinical psychoanalysis of racism still then needs to be subjected to a critical reading to ensure that it locates these processes historically, as with any phenomenological account (cf. Couve, 1986). During the last years of apartheid, some of the good clinical work carried out by psychotherapists working in a psychoanalytic framework did actually include an element of teaching, because traumatized youth in the black townships needed to be able to understand what the 'unconscious' was in order for psychoanalytic psychotherapy to function for them (Straker, 1988). The operation of the Truth and Reconciliation Commission then operated on a psychotherapeutic discourse in which 'trauma' had to be taken seriously in order that it could be spoken about, and spoken about in such a way that the speaking subject believed that it would be cathartic to have done so (Hayes, 1998). Here you can see the importance of ideas about 'catharsis' in early psychoanalysis and the way these early notions have percolated into popular discourse.

Conclusions

Research in the field of psychoanalysis should then be concerned with the way forms of language construct psychoanalytic phenomena as if they were true. Recent close analysis of Freud's own case histories, for example, has shown how the process of 'repression' can be understood as a series of rhetorical strategies, in which someone talks about something in order to avoid something else (Billig, 1999). And this work is complemented by analyses of the way different varieties of psychoanalysis circulate in culture as forms of discourse that produce 'psychoanalytic subjects' (Parker, 1997). What we take to be 'psychopathological', then, needs to become an object of critical research in psychology, not so much in order to do better clinical work, but in order to understand something of how we have become the kind of subjects we so deeply feel ourselves to be.

These ways of using psychoanalysis critically do not necessarily make for a 'critical psychoanalysis', and we should still take care to subject this use of psychoanalysis to critical inquiry. We might read these attempts to use psychoanalysis in such a way as to use and abuse it while treating it as a cultural form, not a part of ourselves, as driven by an impossible relation with it as something 'extimate'. It is intimately bound up with our own experience, but it lies outside, and that is where it should stay. These ways of using psychoanalysis do help us to work in and against the discipline of Psychology, and in and against psychoanalysis to stop it turning itself into another form of psychology, and to bring it closer to critical psychology.

3 The place of transference in psychosocial research

Psychoanalysis is often used by researchers in the emerging field of psychosocial studies as a conceptual and methodological framework that can extrapolate theoretically framed accounts from the clinic to other social contexts. Psychoanalysis provides a complex discursive matrix for making sense of, or unravelling the existing sense of, textual material in social research. However, the relationship between psychoanalytic work in the clinic and psychoanalytic social research poses a series of questions for those working in each domain. The relationship opened up new fields of enquiry, of empirical and theoretical research, but it also now gives rise to empirical and theoretical problems.

This chapter turns directly to look at a key methodological device – 'transference' – that underpins much work in psychosocial research. You will see here how an attention to the reflexivity of the research in qualitative psychology is being 'psychologized', turned into something that a new generation of psychoanalytic psychologists take for granted as something that pre-exists their own inquiries.

The chapter distinguishes three versions of transference in the psychoanalytic tradition, drawing attention to the importance of an 'intersubjective' conception of transference in psychosocial research as an alternative to 'attachment' models that appeal to mainstream empiricist approaches to psychological inquiry. The third version of transference elaborated in Lacanian psychoanalysis, one concerned with signification, is used to ground an analysis of the clinic as the specific space in which the phenomenon manifests itself. Analysis of the clinic as 'transferential space' enables us to conceptualize the place of psychoanalysis in the clinic and to question the extrapolation of transference to social research. The chapter concludes with a consideration of 'generalized transference' outside the clinic to try to account for the appeal of the notion of 'transference' to those in psychosocial studies.

Psychoanalysis faces a problem that arises from its apparent success as an interpretative paradigm. The problem is that what was once thought to be particular to clinical practice has become universalized, and this by way of a surreptitious infiltration of psychoanalytic explanation through the human sciences so that it functions as an interpretive matrix that confirms the shape of a world it expects to find instead of changing it – and this problem may even be said to afflict those who use psychoanalysis with radical intent (e.g. Hollway and Jefferson, 2000; Clarke and Hoggett, 2009).

The emergence of psychosocial research as a distinct field of conceptual and empirical work promises to connect our understanding of the individual with an exploration of social processes, but the use of psychoanalysis as a dominant framework has been contentious (Frosh and Baraitser, 2008). The role of transference as a motif in this research is particularly indicative of the problematic role of psychoanalytic theory, particularly use of the work of Melanie Klein (1986). The term 'transference' in this research is used to describe the way significant relationships from the past, of an interviewee for example, are replicated in the intersubjective space of the interview, and it is assumed that these past relationships are communicated to the researcher, who then attends to them as their own 'counter-transference'. Proponents of psychosocial research now argue, for example, that interview material can be interpreted in terms of 'unconscious intersubjective dynamics' and they include illustrative focus on the case of 'mother and daughter transferences and counter-transferences' (Hollway and Jefferson, 2000: 52). In this work there is the claim that transference and counter-transference can be deployed to make sense of social phenomena (Hollway, 2008). These are the methodological cornerstones of a theory of the 'defended subject' (Hollway and Jefferson, 2000), one which privileges Kleinian psychoanalysis.

In psychosocial research this deployment of transference has two aspects. The first appears in speculation about transference operating for a subject of research outside an interview, in the claim that, in the case of one interviewee called 'Vince', 'It is possible there was transference from the father figure to the boss (both of whom he described as frightening) once he felt let down by him, just as his father let him down' (Hollway and Jefferson, 2005: 159). The second aspect appears in an attention to the feelings of the researcher which is warranted by using the notion of 'counter-transference', as where Hollway remarks on the significance of what is said by way of what is 'revealed in the counter-transference responses of the researcher" (Hollway and Jefferson, 2005: 151).

This use of transference and counter-transference in critical qualitative research in psychology is quite recent. The term 'transference' appears in the foreword to a reissued edition of the classic text *Changing the Subject* by Henriques *et al.* (1998), but did not appear in the first (1984) edition, neither was it explicitly used in Hollway's (1989) exploration of research dynamics in interviews with heterosexual couples. There have been other attempts to configure the research interview as a therapeutic enterprise and to put transference to work in that context (e.g. Kvale, 1996), but the new wave of psychosocial research turns transference into a defining principle of reflexive inquiry; as one contribution puts it, 'placing the counter-transference of the researcher at the centre of our attempt to understand the researched as revealed in the interplay of defended intersubjectivity' (Froggett and Wengraf, 2004: 118–119).

In this chapter I will focus on the way transference – the key process that frames and powers work in the clinic – operates in this kind of interpretative matrix, and show how a Lacanian take on these issues may well be part of the problem, but can also help us find a way out of it. Lacan's (2006) innovative return to Freud shifted focus from biologically wired-in processes that emphasize the attachment of infant to mother and circumvented humanist alternative readings that stress intersubjective processes of meaning-making. Instead, Lacan drew attention to the importance of language in the psychoanalytic cure, and thereby opened the way to a form of psychoanalytic theory that is critical of the reduction of explanation to the level of individual psychology (Parker, 2003a, 2003b). Lacanian psychoanalysis does also risk operating as a powerful metanarrative that makes exaggerated claims to provide a correct interpretation of social phenomena, though it should be noted that Lacan did not himself use the notion of transference when he engaged in wider social theory (Lacan, 1991/2007). A strategic deployment of a Lacanian approach to transference can enable us to locate transference in the clinic and to question the ideological effects of psychoanalysis in contemporary culture.

The task of tracing consequences of the misapplication of clinical concepts is here driven by three imperatives in social research: first, to respect the specificity of different distinct sites of practice, to treat each institutional domain as operating according to a distinct logic by which it is structured and reproduces itself; second, to attend to particular forms of subjectivity that inhere in and arise from each historically constituted domain of work; third, to develop modes of analysis that are tailored to explicate, illuminate and transform determinate social relations. There are therefore issues here to do with the spatial, temporal and analytical specificity of psychoanalysis as a clinical practice and the role of Lacanian theory as an enabling force and false path to our work.

Versions of transference

First it is necessary to distinguish different versions of transference in psychoanalysis. We can then appreciate the way psychosocial research operates with particular conceptions of transference and counter-transference. In contemporary psychosocial research the term 'counter-transference' is used to refer to 'feelings' that cue the researcher into what they think is occurring between them and their objects of study. A quite specific notion of transference is therefore being put to work, one that Lacan's contribution to psychoanalysis can tease apart. A very schematic summary of different traditions, using Lacanian concepts to make sense of the differences between them, here highlights the role of the 'imaginary', the 'symbolic' and the 'real'. We will return to these concepts later in the chapter when we turn to the construction of 'transferential space', but it will help the argument now to briefly explicate what Lacan means by these concepts.

The 'symbolic' is the field of structured meanings that each individual subject has to negotiate to communicate with others, and it includes not only language as such but the broader range of semiotic material – images, sounds, gestures – that human beings inhabit as the necessary if contradictory architecture of culture (Lacan, 1953). An attention to the series and systems of 'signifiers' that comprise the symbolic might be said to bring Lacanian psychoanalysis closer to a 'materialist' account of mental processes than an idealist one which attempts to ground its account in invisible meanings inside the heads of individuals, closer perhaps to a 'concrete psychology' (Politzer, 1994). However, human beings communicate with each other on the necessarily mistaken basis that there is 'understanding' between them which seems to operate independently of signifiers, outside the symbolic. This realm of understanding is the 'imaginary', and it hosts a range of human capacities for empathy and fellow-feeling that is grounded in the presence of each subject to another, paradigmatically in face-to-face interaction. Lacan (1975/1991) abandoned early positive references to 'intersubjectivity' in his work to a more critical account of the 'imaginary' lure into complete understanding of the other that it entails. One might say that the imaginary supports the experience of inhabiting a 'reality' that is structured by the symbolic, and this 'reality' as a conventionalized commonsensical field of meaning – the symbolic – is given its own peculiar coloration by our own idiosyncratic, imaginary, take on it. Lacan distinguishes this 'reality' from what he calls the 'real', and this 'real' may be conceptualized as completely outside any meaningful frame of reference, operating as a traumatic surplus of reality that cannot be symbolized (Lacan, 1964/1973). What should be noted here is that the 'real' is not reducible to the empirical realm that psychology attempts to describe.

Each competing tradition in psychoanalysis provides its own origin story for the appearance of transference as obstacle and opportunity for clinical work. So, it is worth rehearsing the way different conceptions of transference give warrant to the interpretation of social phenomena and the position of a researcher working outside the clinic. There is an important shift in Freud's own writing: from viewing transference as an inconvenient displacement of intensity from unconscious representations to conscious ideas (which may include the figure of the analyst and thus serve as resistance to the cure), it is then seen as an inevitable and necessary part of the process of psychoanalysis, so inevitable and necessary that, after Freud's death, there has been much discussion among psychoanalysts over how to install the transference (Laplanche and Pontalis, 1988).

Transferences, Freud argues, are 'facsimiles' of fantasies of the analysand given new life and new objects, and these facsimiles were later complemented in some accounts by what were termed the 'counter-transference' responses of the analyst (Freud, 1915; Heimann, 1950). Overlapping debates over the nature of counter-transference include speculation as to whether it is a fancy name for the analyst's transference, whether it is what is provoked in the analyst by the analysand's transference, whether it is an aspect of the transference that includes analyst and analysand, or whether it provides a means for accessing the unconscious of analyst and analysand. The role of counter-transference within transference now gives to transference itself a particular hue in different psychoanalytic traditions, as can be seen in debates over the role of counter-transference between Kleinian and Lacanian psychoanalysts (e.g. Hinshelwood, 1997; Palomera, 1997).

There is, first, a tradition of work that views psychoanalysis as always having been concerned with some form of *attachment* between infant and mother, and then by implication between adult human beings, including those in psychoanalysis. The guiding motif of this model of development is that such early bonding is, in one way or another, evolutionarily wired into the formation of love relationships. The relationship between analysand and analyst then replays not only ontogenetic patterns but also resonates with the phylogenetic account elaborated by Freud concerning events in the primal horde, for example. This model of transference is of it as a special kind of glue holding people together, and it is of a piece with specifications of what the infant is presumed to already know of the world they are born into and with research using brain scans to discover which bits of the brain light up when attachment is activated (Fonagy and Target, 2004).

We could say that this overall covering explanation of transference, which treats it as a particular subset of the attachment of the subject to their objects, operates somewhere between the imaginary – complementary relationships which we all experience with our others – and the real. However, this 'real' is an imaginarized version of the real; rather than that which is resistant to representation and impossible to access – the Lacanian real – this real is conceived as something that can be observed or reconstructed by researchers. This tradition, which spans the imaginary and the real, encompasses a range of positions, in which we will find an assortment of Kleinians along with avowedly developmentalist contemporary Freudians (Fonagy *et al.*, 2004; Stern, 1985). This first tradition of work is usually far too reductive for psychosocial researchers, and it tends to underpin modes of research that correspond with traditional psychology (Cushman, 1991). We need to turn to a second tradition in order to grasp what is appealing about the notion of transference for the new school of more critical 'psychosocial' researchers today.

The second tradition has come to value what is *intersubjective* in the psychoanalytic relationship, and focuses on what intuitive responses on the part of the analyst may tell the analyst, and potentially also the analysand, about what is going on between them. The guiding motif of this approach is that the relational dimension of human activity also operates as a kind of conduit for feelings that can be accessed by partners in the relationship. This means that what is intersubjective is given not only epistemological but also moral value, and so the analyst who is able to work with their own counter-transference is therefore assumed to be actualizing some of the deepest unconscious communication flowing from the analysand. This kind of communication also often bypasses the realm of representation to work directly with feelings.

This tradition provides an overall covering account for transference that operates somewhere along a dimension running between the imaginary and the symbolic. Here, however, this symbolic is not a structured system of signifying processes that operates independently of the subject – the Lacanian symbolic – but is, instead, a realm of communicational material in which each subject is embedded and through which they might discover their shared humanity. This is the symbolic as the domain of common sense, which gives to this account of transference a particular appeal. This tradition again spans a range of approaches, which include many object-relations analysts, as well as relational and intersubjective analysts and those from

Jungian analytical psychology who have rejoined the psychoanalytic fold (e.g. Fairfield *et al.*, 2002; Samuels, 1993b). Klein's (1986) work is then read through the optic of this tradition as if it operates as a form of object-relations theory.

The third tradition concerns itself with the *signifying* operations through which human beings come to be positioned in relation to each other and through which they struggle to position themselves. This Lacanian tradition will be employed and elaborated in more detail through the rest of the chapter as a counterpoint to the intersubjective tradition and as a point of leverage to understand the limitations of it. In this third tradition transference is defined by the repetition of signifiers; those that will be of specific value to the analysand and which appear in their speech as they produce a representation of themselves to the analyst, and those that appear and reappear in the language of the analysis, and here include the signifiers introduced into the analysis by the analyst as well as the analysand (cf. Lacan, 1960–1961). The analyst tries to avoid appeal to a domain of feelings hidden beneath the signifiers (or inside the analyst in a separate domain of counter-transference) or recourse to a 'metanarrative' that would provide a point of escape from their effects (or a place from which the transference could be interpreted to the analysand who remains trapped within it). It is materialist insofar as it attends only to the actual signifiers and their position in relation to the system of signifiers in the analysis, materialist insofar as it is a 'concrete psychology' that does not treat the unconscious or other such phenomena as hidden spectres that guide human activity (Dunker and Parker, 2009).

We can say of this third tradition – which includes that of Lacanian psychoanalysis – that it is located somewhere between the symbolic and the real. The imaginary functions as a lure of self-identity, identification and miscommunication that sustains the kinds of psychoanalysis that have attempted to bypass forms of representation and have instead succumbed to biologized and psychologized representations of human relationships (in the first two traditions I have described). However, we should note that this third tradition also spans the symbolic and the real in such a way as to include a number of different competing approaches, various figures claiming the legacy of Lacan (e.g. Gueguen, 1995; Soler, 1996a).

Constructions of transferential space

It could be said that speaking to another under transference is what defines psychoanalysis, that it is the most minimal single condition for there to be psychoanalysis. Here I argue that this transference is precisely what pertains precisely and specifically to the clinic. By 'clinic' I mean a delimited space of work dedicated to the production of a certain kind of speech, and that means that this space is to some extent enclosed and private. It is not necessary that the one who speaks does this in an expensively decorated apartment or a hygienic hospital side-room, and we know that Freud, for example, sometimes conducted analyses while strolling along in the countryside (Gay, 1988). We have accounts of this 'clinic' structured in such unlikely locations as a South African township under apartheid (Straker, 1994), even on long-distance phone lines from the United States (Fink, 2007). This delimited space of work signifies to those speaking that psychoanalysis is taking place in such a way that transference can be activated. How does it do that?

These seven characteristics of the psychoanalytic clinic conducive to transference cluster together in different ways, with different weighting depending on the distinctive tradition in which those who speak have been schooled. A Lacanian perspective is useful as a counterpoint to the tradition of research in psychosocial studies that attends to 'counter-transference' because Lacan attends to interactional space as constituted by signifiers, constituted as what I term here 'transferential space'. I will draw out some contrasts with social research, including psychoanalytic research, and here I am concerned mainly with those forms of research that do actually embed the researcher in a relationship between speaking subjects, though I will comment on other kinds of research that appeal to the notion of transference in the reading of texts towards the end of this review of characteristics of the kind of speech that defines transference.

Analysis is sustained by a commitment to speak that is marked by payment on the part of the one who speaks.

The first peculiarity of transferential space is that the analysand should make a request for analysis, and pay to speak to the analyst. There have been exceptions to this rule – that it is necessary for the analysand to give something to the one they speak to – but the very fact that they are exceptions serves to prove the rule. That psychoanalysis requires commodity exchange does, of course, draw attention to psychoanalytic practice as intimately bound up with capitalism. This was, in fact, one of the grounds for prohibiting analysis in Eastern Europe before the fall of the Wall, for it was seen as a form of private entrepreneurship that ran against the ethos of public health provision (M. Miller, 1998).

The question of how the demand for analysis would be marked, if not by the usual fee, was one that exercised those involved in the public clinics run by psychoanalysts in the early years in Vienna. We find great variation in practice over the years, and there are accounts of Freud waiving fees or lending his patients money in times of hardship, and there were even arrangements made by psychoanalytic institutions to give financial support to well-known patients, the Wolf Man for example (Gardiner, 1972).

Disputes over how much should be paid, when exactly the time starts and finishes, and whether that payment includes sessions missed by the analysand or holidays taken by the analyst, are grist to the mill of transference. The transference does, to some extent, revolve around such matters, but the point here is that this material exchange – money for what; certainly not for many words in return – is one of the material conditions for transference. Surveys of therapists working in private practice have shown that such therapists do, rather unsurprisingly, see payment as more important to the work than those working in public health settings, but even this motif of the self-interested therapist rationalizing an aspect of their practice is the least of it (Power and Pilgrim, 1990). The analysand makes an investment, a material investment in the analytic process, and it is within this investment that many other kinds of transferential investment in the analyst will be constructed and revealed.

It should be noted here that this first defining characteristic of transference is precisely the reverse of the position of a researcher who may want to use psychoanalytic theory to interpret their field of study. Even a psychosocial researcher who is keen to recruit subjects may pay them to speak, but it is unthinkable that their subjects will pay them for the pleasure of participating in a research project.

Potent cues, extrinsic and intrinsic, indicate what should be included in the content of analytic speech.

A second characteristic of transferential space is that there is some expectation that certain things will be spoken about, and a stereotypical list will include childhood, dreams and sexual fantasies. The content of the speech provides a series of opportunities for staging and reflecting upon relationships to others, and the combination between the different aspects of the speech produces a reorganization of the speech around the one it is addressed to. It is not absolutely necessary, for example, that the analysand talks about their childhood, and there are a series of little traps for those who look to accurate representation of childhood events as the aim of analysis (Burman, 1998).

Freud's own writings show an increasing focus on memories of childhood, from the early case histories, where there is scarcely any connection made between hysterical symptomatology and actual or fantasized childhood events, to later studies in which anthropological research is used to direct more attention to childhood development through the rhetorical device of claiming that ontogeny recapitulates phylogeny. The motif of the child grows in importance after Freud's death, and the turn to pre-Oedipal and attachment phenomena, even those that could be empirically observed (Miller *et al.*, 1989). Nevertheless, in both classical and Lacanian psychoanalysis, it is the representation of childhood that is of concern, not what actually happened there and then. It is precisely the attention to the representation of childhood relationships that cues analysand and analyst into how such relationships are replayed in the present.

Dreams are then indexed to the past, with childhood providing the most potent of the scenes to be rediscovered not only in the dream itself but in the retelling of the dream to another. And this figure as other, addressee of the speech of the analysand, becomes the one who may be the only one to hear of sexual fantasies, or perhaps even of the lack of such fantasies and associated threads of guilt and shame at their appearance or non-appearance in the life of the analysand. Not every analytic session revolves around childhood memories or dreams or sexual fantasy, and rarer still will be sessions that combine those topics in such a way as to draw attention to where the speech is coming from and to the point at which it may be directed. However, the circling around those connections and their points of address is the stuff of analysis and so also, in a way very different from everyday conversation, the stuff of transference.

Again, we should note that whether or not a researcher is willing to listen to such things, their own shopping list of topics will only ever accidentally overlap with the content of speech in analysis. A psychosocial researcher may be eager to hear about such things in an interview, but the particular constellation of things that could be expected to appear in analysis and the intense focus on each of them would be most bizarre in a research interview.

Analytic speech is asymmetrical, constituting distinctive positions for addressor and addressee.

The third defining characteristic of transferential space is that there are quite precise formal properties of the speech, for there is an explicit rule which the analysand, who speaks most of the time, is expected to attempt to follow, as well as implicit rules that the analyst follows in their own interventions. The analysand does not follow the normal rules of conversation, but is invited to attempt the impossible, to follow the fundamental technical rule of free association by which they should say everything that comes to mind, however irrelevant, ridiculous or unpleasant. Meandering indirect superfluous speech is sometimes tolerated in everyday life, either of those to be accommodated because they are pitied, or humoured because they are in positions of power, but the assumption in either case – that they enjoy the sound of their own voice and respectful silence will give them some satisfaction – does not hold in analysis. Not only do hesitations, blockages and failures of speech sabotage the attempt to speak, but the satisfaction of speaking is disrupted as the analysand comes to realize that their difficulty in saying everything is localized, organized around certain symptomatic points (Fink, 1997; Nobus, 2000).

The content of analytic speech is important insofar as some things are circled around, and some things will be treated as extraneous and only of interest insofar as they are understood to be opportunities for circling around something else, which is the real core of the analysis. And the analyst will be attending to those moments where the speech stumbles and stops, taking absence as much as any positive content as a sign that at some level the analysand is aware of who they talking to, or unaware of who they are not talking to. They are caught in transference, not as something immediately present to awareness but as something that structures what appears and disappears in their speech unbeknownst to them.

What appears in analysis is not only an intimation of what is unconscious, and always only the contours of it rather than the stuff itself, but that there is knowledge of it. The divided subject who speaks in analysis, and whose division becomes more apparent as they fail to follow the rule of free association, conjures into the place of the analyst another subject who they imagine is an empathic active listener, another subject as they would like to be, one that is undivided and who knows what it is that they are really trying to say. The analyst does not fill that place, and if they were to do so it would be highly unlikely that this 'subject supposed to know' whose appearance defines the transference would appear. The sometimes bare, cryptic allusive interventions of the analyst in this necessarily asymmetrical relationship do not comment on 'transference' as such because it would replace ambiguities in the speech of the analysand with a relationship defined by the analyst; there is therefore an avoidance of precisely the kind of clarification of meaning that drives much normal interaction (Klotz, 1995).

The kind of staging, framing, justification, realignment, reassurance, reviewing, debriefing work that a researcher is expected to engage in is necessarily absent in analysis. A psychosocial researcher is committed by virtue of their research position to engage in such a process, and they then make it quite impossible for other qualities of the relationship to appear, qualities of the analytic relationship such as transference that are elicited by virtue of that absence.

A spatial disjunction in the analytic frame magnifies the reflexive implication of the subject in their own speech.

A fourth characteristic of transferential space is engineered by the use of an apparatus, the couch, and this apparatus frames the relationship between analysand and analyst in such a way as to frustrate attempts at open, direct and transparent communication between the two of them. The apparatus itself takes slightly different forms in different kinds of practice, and Lacanians are notoriously cautious about moving from face-to-face sessions to use of the couch, and they may extend the period of what are known as the 'preliminary meetings' to many months or even years. This is because such a speaking position for the analysand is so peculiar and productive of paranoiac phenomena that not every subject is able to bear or make use of it.

There is actually very little theoretical rationale for the use of the couch in Freud's own writing, and he is reported to have said that he started to put his analysands on the couch because he was sick of being stared at for so many hours a day, and so the role of the couch as an 'apparatus' has been explored by sociologists of scientific knowledge to show how this device comes to shape what analysts then report of their work to others (Mangabeira, 1999). In this complaint there is, of course, a clue as to what is operating as something reassuring for the analysand when speaking directly to the analyst and observing their reactions to what they say. That form of communication has the effect of prioritizing the line of the imaginary – in which the other is empathic partner or rivalrous counterpart in dialogue – over the symbolic. It is the symbolic through which the subject travels as they become other to themselves and which the speaking subject in analysis now attends to as they hear themselves borrow from the symbolic forms that have come to define who they are and repeat the signifiers that compose it.

The couch itself has been an object of psychoanalytic inquiry, with some discussion of how analysands make use of it, whether they may go to sleep on it, for instance, or whether they might fall off it (e.g. Waugaman, 1987). Particular interpretations might be made of such things, but the risk here is that the apparatus itself is being concretized, rather than attention being directed to the strange relationship between speaker and listener that is facilitated by it. The strangeness of that relationship is what is aimed at by most analysts, including by Lacanians, when they discuss, for example, the degree to which analysis over the telephone might or might not serve the same purpose, or whether the embodied presence, absent to sight, of the analyst is necessary to produce a space that is more than imaginary, that is distinctively psychoanalytic, as a condition of transference.

The use of the couch as an apparatus in psychosocial interview research is, of course, quite unusual, however much the researcher may want to use psychoanalytic theory to make sense of what is said in the interview. The material construction of the relationship that psychoanalysis has developed is therefore not operative in psychosocial research.

Specific performative effects of the analyst's speech elicit, guide and frame what is said to them.

The transferential space of analysis depends, fifth, on the activity of the analyst, who adopts a rather strange position from the beginning of the interaction, and whose function is to intensify and manage the analytic work through specific kinds of intervention. The analyst does not direct the analysand to speak about particular things but, in Lacan's well-known formulation, 'directs the treatment' (Lacan, 1958). This contrast between quite different conceptions of how the course of the analysis will be framed and guided has consequences for how interpretation, including interpretation of the transference, will be made. Interpretation does not aim to excavate particular contents or to produce a certain kind of knowledge; rather than being descriptive it aims to bring about certain effects; it is performative. One of the problems faced by the analyst is that an increasing number of analysands are themselves schooled in psychoanalytic theory, and ready to anticipate the kinds of interpretations that might be produced in the space of analysis.

Recent debates about the changing cultural-historical conditions for analysis have included reflection on the degree to which interpretation is itself a form of activity through which the unconscious maintains itself, and which the analyst may only feed if they respond to the speech of the analysand by providing more interpretations. These debates have resulted in ever more sparse interventions by Lacanian analysts, to the point where the aim of an intervention is directed to the 'cutting' and disruption of the self-satisfied interpretative speech of the analysand, rather than the feeding of the unconscious and so the feeding of forms of defence (Miller, 1999).

Lacanians have long argued that while it is necessary to work in the transference – for it is an essential condition of analysis itself – interpretation of the transference can be tantamount to suggestion, and so should be avoided as a rule (Burgoyne, 1997). Interpretation of transference, when it is made, does not then serve to locate analysand and analyst in a certain relationship, conceived as the repetition of a past relationship, but to disrupt what may be understood to be occurring between the two of them (Cottet, 1993). Interpretation does not, in any case, aim to produce better understanding but to disturb that understanding. One of the consequences of such interventions is to throw into question all the more so than before the kind of knowledge that would be expected from analysis. This serves to emphasize Lacan's argument that signifiers be reduced to nonsense in analysis rather than given any meaning, or form of understanding that could then be given to the analysand (Nobus and Quinn, 2005). It is the relation to knowledge that comes to assume more importance than any knowledge as such, and so we are in the realm of performative effects rather than the production of new ideas or moral prescriptions.

The psychosocial researcher therefore has to make a choice which is defined by the position they adopt as a researcher rather than as an analyst. Apart from the distinctive form of silence the analyst constructs around the words of the analysand, their actual interventions have a performative quality. This is out of the question in mainstream social research, though 'action research' would be an instance where there is an attempt to change the world while interpreting (e.g. Martín-Baró, 1994); to change social relations by way of consciousness-raising rather than the inculcation of subjects into psychoanalytic discourse. The researcher has a responsibility to guide the speech of their subject, but in a way that the analyst deliberately avoids; if a researcher were to interpret a subject's response of transference they would risk installing them in an imaginary relationship prone to suggestion, as Lacan warns.

Speech in analysis has a counter-intuitive temporality designed to question everyday conversational procedures.

A sixth characteristic of transferential space is its disturbing temporal quality, and it is by virtue of this quality that another dimension of thought is opened up which breaks from consciousness, which is typically structured by way of obedience to rational linear and predictable clock-time (Lacan, 1975/1991). Lacanians return to some of the earliest procedures of psychoanalysis, before the advent of the tidy fifty-minute hour. Freud's wife Martha described how she liked to water the plants in the consulting room every hour, and needed about ten minutes to do this, and so it has been suggested that it was from this that fifty minutes a session became the ideal length for the famous analytic hour (Schmideberg, 1971). Psychoanalysis breaks from clock-time to more closely track the time of the unconscious, and it is for this reason that Lacanians interfere with the temporal space of analysis to open up the unconscious.

A neatly structured analytic session that ends at a pre-determined time, for example, enables the analysand to predict and pace their speech according to a logic that is ordered by the clock and commanded by consciousness. Such conscious strategies of measured speech are sabotaged by the analyst who ends the session earlier, or perhaps sometimes later, than expected. The ending of such a session – the famous variable-length Lacanian session – may itself function as an interpretation, and such an interpretation which marks a point of some significance in the analysand's speech has the advantage of not spelling out what the exact meaning of that point may be. One may think of the end of this kind of session as setting in place an uncompleted task for the analysand, and the very ambiguity of the point of the ending may produce a question to be taken up in a later session (Burgoyne, 1997).

Such tactics also bring into play a retroactive characteristic of analysis that repeats the retroactive character of traumatic events, and that retroactivity is a template for every other kind of experience in which the unconscious is at work. So, the organization of the space for speech in analysis is designed to draw attention to the role of the unconscious, to make this space into a setting where the phenomenon of transference can appear, where it makes sense to feel that what is being repeated and reactivated after the event in the speech also repeats and reactivates something from the past of the speaker in relation to the one they are speaking to (Soler, 1996b).

Once again, the psychosocial researcher has to conform to linear procedures that an analysand comes to question as they reflect on how their own present is borne by the past. To break from linear time is to break from every protocol demanded by ethics committees in the field of social research, protocols designed to avoid lawsuits for their institutions. Not only will the speaking subject in analysis speak about things outside any contract, beyond what they have given their permission to be included, they will not know when they will say it or what it may mean until it is too late. In this way another defining characteristic of transferential space is precluded in psychosocial research, and so it no longer makes sense to employ the notion of transference or counter-transference.

Analytic speech requires address to, and response from, another.

I have left this condition until last, until seventh; for it is here that we encounter the reflexive looping that positions the analysand in relation to the analyst as they speak, but also that which positions the analyst in relation to the subject who is speaking to them when they produce interpretations. It is this reflexive looping which ties analyst to analysand that a psychoanalytic social researcher tends to mischaracterize when they are in the presence of subjects who speak to them and that they bypass when they confine themselves to textual material that cuts out the response of any speaking subject whatsoever.

This condition is actually the prerequisite for the other six, because analysis must take place in a relationship – or we should say 'non-relationship' – between speaking beings (Wright, 1999). Psychoanalytic interpretations are made to another subject for whom they function more by way of the response to the interpretation being made than with reference to its content. And, in many cases, the interpretations are made not by the analyst but by the analysand themselves, or they are interventions that come to take the form of interpretations as the analysand refuses or reconfigures what was said by the analyst, sometimes quite a while after the event.

It might be argued that the transferential position of the researcher is at work not through their activity as analyst – in which the ethnographic, documentary or interview transcript might be treated as if it were a kind of analysand – but that the researcher is themself a kind of analysand (e.g. Hollway and Jefferson, 2005). Here, the reasoning might be that the form of transferential bond that is forged with the material is more akin to what is sometimes termed 'counter-transference'. Note here that there is the separation off of counter-transference as something distinct from transference itself, a move that Lacan contested (Lacan, 1952), and this separation lands us with more problems in social research. Here the motif of transference is imported into research under the guise of 'counter-transference' and, at the same time, there is another lure, for it is as if it is a supercharged, more reflexive form of transference because it is the kind of transference that an analyst would have to the material.

The claim that the researcher may employ their 'counter-transference' to make sense of a text of some kind actually compounds the problem. What this surreptitious appeal to something more than bare transference overlooks is that there is no subject speaking, no subject with which and against which any interpretations are elaborated and contested.

Generalized transference and its effects

The conditions for any kind of transference are missing, though there are perhaps other kinds of process that are themselves of psychoanalytic interest and that might help us to think through why such researchers would come to believe there was transference at work in the first place. There are a number of aspects of conceptual leakage from the clinic into research that we need to take into account in order to give a theoretical account of the way this conceptual leakage turns transference into what we could term 'generalized transference' in contemporary culture. I will note three aspects here.

Psychologization of subjectivity

First, there is an increasing psychologization of individual subjectivity, and then of the way that social processes are understood using that psychologized individual experience as a theoretical template. By psychologization I mean the reduction of social processes to the level of the individual subject and the induction of that subject into an understanding of themselves in which psychological explanations take precedence (Parker, 2007a). That psychologization commences with the birth of capitalism, and is in fact a necessary condition for capitalism based on commodity exchange to work. Not only does each worker enter into the contract to exchange their labour time for money as if it were of their own free will, but the entrepreneurial activities of the capitalist provide a model for thriving competitive individualism that seeks to maximize profit. Psychologization is necessary through the development of capitalism as the material ideological texture of everyday life, through which economic mechanisms appear to be grounded in the survival of the fittest, and it has become all the more important in times of neoliberal deregulation of welfare services and intensification of precarious entrepreneurial labour conditions, in which the worker is now also an entrepreneur.

Despite the difference between psychology and psychoanalysis, and with the popular conflation of psychology and psychoanalysis as symptomatic of the problem, the circulation of psychoanalytic representations of the self is part and parcel of this process of psychologization. Whatever the subversive potential of psychoanalysis in the clinic or in social theory, psychoanalytic vocabulary has seeped into psychologized accounts of individual and social activity in everyday life. The subversive potential of the clinic is debatable, and the reduction of its horizons to change to the individual – 'one by one', it is said in some Lacanian circles – does not augur well. We need to contend with the way contemporary psychologization is itself a form of academicization in which the academic tries to interpret and touch a real world of their fantasy 'outside' the university (De Vos, 2008). Here, generalized transference operates as an implicit conceptual category that is used by social researchers positioned as academics commenting upon the networks of relationships and investments in relationships, phenomena that they detect in others. It operates, then, as a pathologizing account in which the position of the researcher is cunningly excluded, and so this is psychoanalytic research conducted as if were a metalanguage. That is, psychosocial research is willing to attend to 'reflexivity' only insofar as their reflections give them insight into what their subjects are thinking and feeling; their 'counter-transference' then has the status of a metalanguage which explains what is really going on. This is not to say that the inclusion of the researcher in the account would necessarily be better, which brings us to the second aspect of generalized transference.

Psychotherapeutic framing of analysis

Second, there is a process of recuperation of psychoanalysis into a particular model of clinical practice that then also provides a particular model of social change; psychoanalysis reduced to psychotherapy becomes concerned with 'feelings' underneath language instead of social relations that are reiterated and reproduced as language itself is used to describe and warrant different kinds of world. The motif of researching 'beneath the surface' in psychosocial research is indicative of this problem (e.g. Clarke and Hoggett, 2009). Psychoanalysis is, on the one hand, often reduced to being a form of psychology – a description of childhood development, personality differences, pathological interpersonal relationships, and so on – but it has also often been reduced to operating as a kind of psychotherapy. The stakes of the difference between psychoanalysis as such and the way it has been reconfigured under conditions of psychologization as a form of psychotherapy are high. To rehearse the psychoanalytic critique of psychotherapy very briefly, we can note the following. There is a questioning by psychoanalysts of the attainment of empathy, and of harmonization between aspects of the self. Psychoanalysts do not aim to dispel illusion, and do not search under the surface of spoken interaction and excavate a deeper reality behind language. They do not educate someone about what is right or wrong or as to how they should understand themselves, or attempt to normalize certain kinds of behaviour or experience. Instead, they attend to how treating certain kinds of behaviour or experience as pathological may merely serve to transform them from things that the analyst may not understand into things they think they understand very well so they can determine what is good and bad for their analysand; they are thereby turned into elements of a moral and moralizing narrative. Psychoanalysts do not render treatment into a process that can be made susceptible to prediction as part of 'evidence-based' practice, nor promote rationality as the touchstone of conscious understanding.

The therapeutic framing of psychoanalysis is relevant to some of the ways that psychoanalysis has been taken up in social research. It is here that all manner of appeals are made to what the researcher feels about the research topic or their relationship to those they include as subjects, and it is here that much talk of 'transference' and 'counter-transference' serves as warrant for supposedly psychoanalytic explanations of social processes. The researcher becomes subject to a 'psychoanalytic culture' in which they deliberately or unwittingly subscribe to psychoanalytic conceptions of subjectivity (Parker, 1997). Here we will indeed find cases of researchers who genuinely experience what they understand to be 'transference', but we need to obey a first rule of psychoanalysis, which is to question how genuine experience is configured and organized not around 'feelings' we think are under the surface because we experience them ourselves but around representations organized within signifying practices, in this case representations of psychoanalysis.

Deference to the clinic

The third aspect of conceptual leakage through which a form of psychoanalysis comes to circulate outside the clinic as generalized transference is the place of the clinic in culture and, as part of this problematic, the place of the clinic for those conducting psychoanalytic social research. There is a good deal of deference to psychoanalytic clinical work that actually does psychoanalysis few favours, even if it is a deference that may itself be cultivated by some practising psychoanalysts. This deference to the clinic is actually at the heart of the problem I have identified in much psychosocial research, and I have been concerned in this chapter with the way the clinic functions as an idealized model of the kind of interpretation those who like psychoanalysis think they should make everywhere else. The privilege given to the clinic is marked in a number of social practices. I shall single out three, and note the function of a form of 'transference' within them.

The first social practice concerns 'pre-transference', and is to be found in a domain of discussions in clinical work that attempts to connect with social processes, that for good sound clinical reasons attempts to embed the actual clinical work in a network of pre-existing cultural processes and structures of power (Kareem and Littlewood, 1999). It is sometimes noted, for example, that an analysand entering analysis for the first time already carries with them preconceptions that will determine how they will relate to the analyst. These preconceptions may even be conceptualized as a kind of 'cultural baggage' that will then determine choices of analyst based on racial or ethnic characteristics, or assumptions about the ways that an analyst of a certain type might treat them. The working assumption may be that there is already transference before the analysis starts. This transference or 'pre-transference' may be to the analysis itself, and may include within it a number of stereotypical representations of what analysis is and anticipation of the forms of repetition of patterns that will take place within it. We should note in this case that there is already an extrapolation from the transferential space of the clinic to other kinds of social space, and also note that this is useful only insofar as that extrapolation is being used retroactively to reconfigure how the actual transference works. The mistake would be to treat transference as operating in the abstract, independently of any psychoanalysis actually taking place.

The second social practice concerns what I will call 'shallow transference', and I use it here to characterize the particular attachment some social researchers have to clinical practice as fund of concepts which they can draw upon in order to understand their own work or to understand the activities of their 'subjects', their objects of inquiry (cf. Wolfe, 1989). There is a degree of idealization of psychoanalysis and privileged sites of interpretation in contemporary culture and so also in social research. These sites operate as anchoring points around which psychoanalysis in the clinic as a particular form of representational practice coheres and these sites provide, at some moments, an illustrative account as to how psychoanalytic practice operates in the popularization of striking case studies, for example. However, 'shallow transference' merely serves to mimic what is imagined to take place inside the clinic, and has its own distinctive characteristics that should not be confused with transference as such. To say that there is transference to transference does not solve the problem, but compounds it, for it obscures the complicated procedures by which subjects are enrolled in research practice and it reduces all of these procedures to psychoanalysis itself as a pre-existing taken-for-granted grid of knowledge. This problem also applies to the third practice, but with a twist, for here researchers have already been inducted into psychoanalysis of some kind and they know deep in themselves that it is true.

The third social practice concerns what I shall term 'hollow transference', and I use this to characterize the enthusiasm of those who have themselves had some intimate engagement with psychoanalysis, in the form of Lacanian psychoanalysis perhaps or some other form of psychoanalysis or psychoanalytic psychotherapy, and use that as their reference point to make sense of social phenomena (cf. Laplanche, 1999). The reference to personal experience in therapy then provides a distinctive problem for those of us trying to disentangle the clinic from political critique, and those who want to conceptualize the intersections between clinical and theoretical psychoanalysis. In this case there is not merely an attraction to psychoanalysis and an image of it as a form of knowledge – as is the case for those already rehearsing psychoanalytic notions in their own lives as 'shallow transference' – but an avid attachment to a transferential space that remains idealized after the event. It would be too simple to say that those enmeshed in such forms of 'hollow transference' have been insufficiently analysed, and such explanation would itself fall back into the idealization of what we might imagine a full or genuine analysis to be.

Close attention to the precise limitations of the concept of 'pre-transference' and to the role of 'shallow transference' and 'hollow transference' among enthusiasts for psychoanalysis in social research is designed to question the role of transference as such outside the clinic. It is designed to warn against us taking transference for granted and simply seeing the clinic as a source of wisdom, and there is also an issue here for clinical training organizations that use the notion of transference as an explanatory device and thereby incite something very like it in the identificatory processes that structure the way they work. Instead, it is the place of the clinic itself that needs to be analysed, needs to be conceptually and empirically examined so that its function as a specific apparatus for the construction and deconstruction of subjectivity can be better understood (Parker, 2009).

Conclusions

There are certain rules of speech, always operative and now governed by ethics committees, that prohibit the researcher from turning their interaction with their 'subjects' into analysis, and so there is no transference. There are everyday norms of interaction that cannot be easily flouted by someone wanting to turn the conversation into analysis, and someone trying to do so would be seen as quite bizarre. Lacanian psychoanalysis draws attention to the specific norms of clinical interventions, and its focus on the signifying material that structures psychoanalytic speech enables us to map the clinic as a quite particular transferential space.

The task is to develop specific modes of analysis that include psychoanalysis itself as a social phenomenon, that do not simply employ psychoanalytic modes of reasoning but that examine how those modes of reasoning have found their way into everyday commonsensical explanations of social and personal life. Some of the interpretative accounts of organizational and cultural processes that simply redefine what is going in psychoanalytic terms succeed not only because the researchers are avid believers in psychoanalysis but also because those who are offered the interpretations in the course of a consultancy or who read the reports in books and journals resonate with those accounts at an experiential level. Those accounts of social processes key in to aspects of personal life history, and such is the tendency of social explanation to be reduced to what individuals in capitalist society share between each other as a common understanding of what individual psychology is that such accounts are reproduced in a self-confirming loop. The very fact that such accounts are felt to be true at a personal level serves to give further intuitive warrant to their status as social, even 'critical', accounts.

There is indeed something like transference at work outside the clinic, and to characterize this as 'generalized transference' does not diminish its effects. The point is that we need to attend to how it operates as a particular phenomenon rather than appeal to transference as such to understand it. It is possible to reinterpret a number of psychoanalytic studies of organizations and culture, and to shift the emphasis from the discovery of underlying psychoanalytic processes, including transference, to the tracing of how psychoanalytic textures of experience, which include generalized transference, are being mobilized by participants. Such research would attend to the situated nature of psychoanalysis through discursive or ethnographic methodological frameworks.

It is here that theoretical reflexive inquiry that pits itself against common sense is imperative. Psychoanalysis outside the clinic has many effects, but the role of transference here, outside the clinic, needs to be carefully examined. There is a weird kind of transference constructed outside the clinic perhaps, but it is not transference as we know it. We need theoretical accounts of the emergence and functions of psychoanalysis in capitalist society that do not simply replicate psychoanalysis itself as if it were a worldview in order to trace the appeal of transference at work in social research.

4 Freud's culture

In this chapter we turn from the realm of clinical treatment to the way that psychoanalysis approaches questions of culture. We have seen from previous chapters that psychoanalysis is a 'talking cure' that is always located in a particular kind of language, the language of the culture that the psychoanalyst needs to have an awareness of in order to practice. The cure requires that there be some sense that things are unconscious to us, pushed out of awareness and kept at bay because they disturb and threaten to undermine what we think makes us happy, and such things also circulate in culture.

Freud homed in on what was most disturbing: sexuality as the most intimate core of who we are and around which we construct hosts of fantasies about how we might love others and find satisfaction in that love. However, one of the lessons of psychoanalysis is that what appears to be most 'intimate' is rooted in our relations with others. In Freud's work there is a cluster of assumptions about the self, and there are complex culturally specific images put to work about what is inside and outside us, what forms of motivation are primary and how they push to the surface, and what speaking about ourselves might cover over or reveal.

This chapter critically reviews Freud's discussions of culture, starting with his arguments for the importance of culture in analytic training, then focusing on his views of collective activity, conceptions of myth and worldviews, the role of politics and religion, connections with his account of civilization, and concluding with consequences that Freud saw for the progress of psychoanalysis itself and for psychoanalysis as part of culture. This gives us a secure base from which to develop psychoanalytically oriented psychosocial studies in a way that is critical of received wisdom.

One of the things we notice about Freud's work over the course of his lifetime is that there is a shift away from individual neurological questions to questions of culture. We can trace the arc of this shift from his earliest work on the aphasias as disorders of language use, in which Freud was already starting to make some connections between neurological disorders and the nature of language itself. Then we find that even at the birth of psychoanalysis there is a necessary separation between biology and culture which is evident in his observation in his visit to Paris in the 1880s that hysteria is not a disorder peculiar to women as traditional psychiatry had it. Psychoanalysis operated on a concept of the 'drive' which, as Freud pointed out, operated at the border of the physiological and the psychical. Mental pain was always infused by cultural processes. Towards the end of his life Freud was less optimistic about the prospects of addressing this pain through individual therapy, and saw psychoanalysis as an approach to understanding the cultural-historical nature of human beings.

There is, in addition, all the way through the early history of psychoanalysis, the history Freud was responsible for shaping through interventions in key debates, a connection between clinical, professional and institutional disputes, and these disputes often connect with political questions. One example is the intense debate over the 'free clinics' and the provision of psychoanalytic treatment to working-class patients who could not afford to pay for consultations with an analyst in private practice. In the debates with Jung over anthropology and literature, Freud honed his skills in interpreting cultural phenomena, and those debates quickly become inflected with a political dimension, one which became salient when the Nazis took power, when psychoanalysis was banned, and when Jung chose to remain at the head of a psychotherapy organization based in Berlin. The debates with Wilhelm Reich (1946/1972) over the connection between psychoanalytic change and political change stretched the conceptual terrain in the other direction, and it does again make clear that psychoanalysis was immersed in cultural-political activities.

These debates have implications for clinical practice, and Freud was clear that psychoanalytic attention to fantasies about abuse, for example, have to be located in the context of abusive family relationships. Against the caricature of psychoanalysis as refusing to acknowledge the reality of child sexual abuse, we find many references in his early writings to the reality of the conditions in which his analysands find themselves. The argument is not that these circumstances are unimportant, but that psychoanalysis has a particular focus on the domain of fantasy. The case descriptions Freud provides have then opened the way to a detailed exploration of the nature of the culture in which the analysand speaks of their distress.

We can see the crucial role of culture in psychoanalysis in Freud's discussions of collective activity, his conception of myth and his comments on the role of worldviews in psychoanalysis. He makes specific comments on politics, religion and civilization, and there are then consequences for how we might understand clinical work. We will begin by looking at what Freud had to say about culture in psychoanalytic training.

Training

In the mid-1920s Freud was embroiled in a series of sharp debates over the role of 'lay analysis'; that is, psychoanalysis carried out by those who were not medically trained. Psychoanalysis in the United States was controlled by doctors, who insisted that a medical training was a prerequisite for analytic training, and this was to have profound consequences for émigré analysts fleeing fascism in Europe. When they arrived in the United States, those who were not medically qualified were not able to practise, and even some of the psychoanalysts who were also doctors had to undergo retraining because their medical qualifications were not recognized. Even the title of Freud's key intervention in these debates is telling. The title 'The Question of Lay Analysis', from which the following quote is taken, was originally translated as 'The Problem of Lay Analysis', which made it seem as if he was arguing alongside the US medics rather than against them.

> If – which may sound fantastic to-day – one had to found a college of psycho-analysis, much would have to be taught in it which is also taught by the medical faculty: alongside of depth-psychology, which would always remain the principal subject, there would be an introduction to biology, as much as possible of the science of sexual life, and familiarity with the symptomatology of psychiatry. On the other hand, analytic instruction would include branches of knowledge which are remote from medicine and which the doctor does not come across in his practice: the history of civilization, mythology, the psychology of religion and the science of literature. Unless he is well at home in these subjects, an analyst can make nothing of a large amount of his material.
>
> (Freud, 1926: 246)

We see a characteristic quality of Freud's writing here which we must take seriously if we want to understand psychoanalysis itself, which is that there is a careful rhetorical positioning of his own standpoint against those he wants to persuade. We will see this again and again in the following extracts. Here we see him posing the possibility of a college that sounds 'fantastic' and in which all of the standard psychiatric topics would need to be taught. Then there is the twist: that, unlike standard psychiatric training, psychoanalysis requires something more, and so it this something more, an attention to culture, that we are invited to see as the defining elements of an authentic psychoanalytic training.

We should note that in Freud's proposal for a college of psychoanalysis he does not suggest that there should be a merging of psychiatry, psychology and cultural studies. Instead, he counterposes a knowledge of biological processes as the kind of thing one might gain in a medical faculty to branches of knowledge that include the history of civilization, mythology, religion and literature. His argument, that the analyst must be 'at home' in these subjects, also has to be understood in the context of quite a sharp divide in German-speaking culture between the realms of the natural sciences and the human sciences. There are, then, consequences for how we should understand collective processes, a topic he had addressed about five years before, and to which we should turn now.

Masses

The title of Freud's 'Group Psychology and the Analysis of the Ego' is, once again, a little misleading, and is a translation of the German title that was more directly concerned with collective phenomena generally. The reference to 'group psychology' already makes it seem as if Freud is proposing an application or extension of individual analysis to a form of 'group analysis', and as if he is concerned here with small groups. In fact, Freud was referring to 'mass psychology', and signalled this in the original title of his book. We should also bear in mind that the phrase 'analysis of the ego' is also quite problematic, and Freud was using an everyday commonsensical term in German ('Ich') to refer to the 'I'. The reference to the 'ego' in the title of his book about mass psychology tends to shift attention away from his theme, which is the immersion of the 'I' in society, to a binary opposition between the individual and the social, an opposition that he was actually questioning:

> The contrast between individual psychology and social or group psychology, which at first glance may seem to be full of significance, loses a great deal of its sharpness when it is examined more closely. It is true that individual psychology is concerned with the individual man and explores the

> paths by which he seeks to find satisfaction for his instinctual impulses; but only rarely and under certain exceptional conditions is individual psychology in a position to disregard the relations of this individual to others. In the individual's mental life someone else is invariably involved, as a model, as an object, as a helper, as an opponent; and so from the very first individual psychology, in this extended but entirely justifiable sense of the words, is at the same time social psychology as well.
>
> (Freud, 1921: 69)

Freud insists here on a relational view of what we might now call the 'subject', pointing out that in the individual's mental life 'someone else is invariably involved', and he then goes on to spell out some of the ways that this 'someone else' might be involved. These implications of 'the other' in the mental life of the subject are then explored in psychoanalytic theory and clinical practice. This formulation differentiates psychoanalysis from 'individual psychology', and so we can see that for Freud psychoanalysis is defined by virtue of its attention to the subject as something always already 'social'. The kind of individual that psychoanalysis is concerned with is one that should be understood through the optic of social psychology.

Freud also neatly turns around a standard view of 'mass psychology', which is the focus of his book, and argues that this kind of mass psychology is not, as is often commonly thought, 'pathological'. Freud's examples in the book include 'crowds', and this aspect is often played up by other writers who are suspicious of crowd behaviour and who look to Freud to support their argument that there is something pathological about collective activity. However, Freud also spends as much time discussing social institutions like the church and the army, and his analysis also refers to parliamentary assemblies. Here we have a range of instances where the subject is in relation to others, and if there is any hint of something 'pathological' in Freud's discussion at this point it is when he refers to the individual, for he says that it is only in 'exceptional conditions' that we are able to disregard the relation of this individual to others.

Myth

Let us go back a few more years in Freud's writing, to one of his case studies – this is from his discussion of the famous case of the 'Wolf Man' – and here we can see how Freud locates the 'Oedipus complex' in an even more complex view of what 'myth' is and how it operates in the individual subject. It is clear here that what we learn from myth is not merely something that is added on to what we know about individual development, but that myth is embedded in the history of the subject. Freud makes reference here to a notion that was current in biological theory and was also being utilized in cultural analysis at the time, which is that 'ontogeny recapitulates phylogeny'; that is, that individual development repeats in miniature the development of the species of which the individual is a member. For example, the human foetus shows at very early stages in its development gill-like mechanisms that testify to the emergence of the human species from an evolutionary sequence that included aquatic creatures:

> . . . the phylogenetically inherited schemata . . . like the categories of philosophy, are concerned with the business of 'placing' the impressions derived from actual experience. I am inclined to take the view that they are precipitates from the history of human civilization. The Oedipus complex, which comprises a child's relation to his parents, is one of them – is, in fact, the best known member of the class. Wherever experiences fail to fit in with the hereditary schema, they become remodelled in the imagination – a process which might very profitably be followed out in detail. It is precisely such cases that are calculated to convince us of the independent existence of the schema. We are often able to see the schema triumphing over the experience of the individual . . .
>
> (Freud, 1918 [1914]: 119)

Problematic as the direct appeal to evolutionary development to explain the functioning of Oedipal structure in human childhood is, Freud's discussion here also presupposes a much more nuanced engagement with cultural and philosophical debates. The mythological structure here operates as a 'schema' that overrides what the individual subject may directly be aware of; Freud says we see 'the schema triumphing over the experience of the individual'. This account thus operates in two ways. On the one hand there is a literal appeal to evolutionary biological processes, and Freud does try to ground the Oedipus complex in events in the 'primal horde' in other writings. On the other hand, however, there is a metaphorical aspect of Freud's argument, and the lesson is that what an individual may report of their 'experience' will not be sufficient to account for the structures that condition who they are, beyond conscious awareness there is something unconscious about the human subject, and this something unconscious is the stuff of myth.

We should not overlook the other cultural reference which Freud alludes to, which is that of the 'categories of philosophy'. These 'categories' are the kinds of schema that the Western Enlightenment philosopher Immanuel Kant describes in his philosophical writings, writings which Freud adverts to in other places, when, for example, he describes the super-ego – that which is 'above-I' – as operating in much the same way as Kant describes the moral 'categorical imperative'. The 'categories' here show us another side to the argument that Freud is making, for alongside the biological evolutionary reference – 'phylogenetically inherited schemata' and suchlike – he is concerned here with the 'placing' of impressions, and if we take the reference to Kant seriously, this 'placing' is in a 'structure' rather than in a series of mythological contents. That is what Oedipus gives us, the description of a 'structure' of relations between infant, care-giver and another figure that intervenes between those first two, not a description of particular culturally specific contents, of babies, mummies and daddies.

Worldviews

In addition to his clinical case histories, theoretical papers and a wide range of studies devoted to literature, history and cultural analysis, Freud took pains to explain psychoanalysis to a wider audience, and his introductory lectures at different points in his career provide valuable insight into how he saw his work intersecting with other fields of study. In the early 1930s, for example, he addressed the hopes that psychoanalysts might have to have their work seen as 'scientific'. There were high stakes here, and we have already noted the division between 'natural sciences' and 'human sciences' in the German-speaking world. Freud does not opt directly for either side of the divide, and it is clear here that he does not see psychoanalysis as providing its own distinct *Weltanschauung* or view of the world:

> Psycho-analysis, in my opinion, is incapable of creating a *Weltanschauung*. It does not need one: it is a part of science and can adhere to the scientific *Weltanschauung*. This, however, scarcely deserves such a grandiloquent title, for it is not all-comprehensive, it is too incomplete and makes no claim to being self-contained and to the construction of systems. Scientific thought is still very young among human beings; there are too many of the great problems which it has not yet been able to solve. A *Weltanschauung* erected upon science has, apart from its emphasis on the real external world, mainly negative traits, such as submission to the truth and rejection of illusions.
>
> (Freud, 1933: 181–182)

There are important lessons here for those who treat psychoanalysis as an overall covering explanation for every aspect of human experience and then try to apply the approach to explain in psychoanalytic terms every other domain. Freud argues that, rather than psychoanalysis developing as a worldview itself, the closest it will come to a worldview is when it operates within a general scientific worldview. However, even this 'worldview' is carefully defined in 'negative' terms, for instead of providing a positive vision of how things are or how things should be, this 'worldview', such as it is, is concerned with 'truth' and 'rejection of illusions'.

There is another problem with the notion of 'worldview' that Freud notes here, another reason why psychoanalysis should be wary of turning itself into a worldview or even participating in a kind of worldview that pretends to provide a complete and inclusive system of knowledge. The problem is that psychoanalysis is 'incomplete' and it makes no claim to provide a 'self-contained' system. We can read this note of caution as also expressing something of the nature of psychoanalytic exploration of contradiction and division. Psychoanalysis does not aim at complete explanation, at a totalizing system of knowledge, but at a relation between the subject and knowledge in which both sides of the equation are defined by their incompleteness.

Politics

Individual and cultural 'worldviews' are anathema to psychoanalysis, and we see this warning once again in Freud's comments on political ideologies. The particular danger arises, he argued, when an ideological system imagines that it is 'self-contained' and 'exclusive'. Freud was politically rather a liberal figure, and viewed with suspicion all grand schemes to change the world. Even so, many of the early psychoanalysts were involved in left or centre-left politics and Freud's comments must be understood against this background. His comment that an enclosed political system like the 'Russian Bolshevism' that he warns against here might turn out to bear an 'uncanny likeness' to what they pit themselves against is not an argument against politics as such, but an argument against 'worldview' politics:

> The newly achieved discovery of the far-reaching importance of economic relations brought with it a temptation not to leave alterations in them to historical development but to put them into effect oneself by revolutionary action. Theoretical Marxism, as realized in Russian Bolshevism, has acquired the energy and the self-contained and exclusive character of a *Weltanschauung*, but at the same time an uncanny likeness to what it is fighting against. Though originally a portion of science and built up, in its implementation upon science and technology, it has created a prohibition of thought which is just as ruthless as was that of religion in the past.
>
> (Freud, 1933: 179–180)

One way of reading this passage is to see Freud inveighing against any attempt to change the world, to see his reference to alterations in 'economic relations' that follow a path of 'historical development' as changes that must be allowed to take their course and not be interfered with by 'revolutionary action'. At the time he was writing, however, there were exactly these kinds of debates occurring among Marxists, and these debates were over the extent to which 'revolutionary action' might substitute for broader political change. The debate concerned tactics and ethics rather than whether change as such should or should not be aimed for.

Likewise, Freud's reference to Marxism as having built itself upon science, as 'originally a portion of science' as he puts it, should be understood within contemporary debates on the Left. There was widespread agreement that a politically progressive scientific worldview, of which Marxism saw itself as a part if not sometimes in the vanguard, would replace archaic regressive religious conceptions of the world. The danger Freud points to is that a closed totalitarian system of thought, which Marxism could itself degenerate into, would then become like a kind of religious system. One can see here echoes of critiques of the Soviet Union that were being developed among Marxists in the 1930s. One thing is clear here, though, and that is Freud's suspicion of religious ideology as such.

Religion

We now go back to one of Freud's early writings – the earliest we will examine here – in which he develops one of his first sustained critiques of religious belief systems. This argument is taken up later in his work at a time when religious mystification has become hitched directly to political debate in the form of fascism, and then we can see him attempt to ground theological notions in detailed historical study. At this early point Freud is arguing from the ground of a 'human science' that would comprehend the development of human civilization, and 'religiosity' would then be symptomatic of a regression at the level of culture and at the level of the individual:

> . . . one might venture to regard obsessional neurosis as a pathological counterpart of the formation of a religion, and to describe that neurosis as an individual religiosity and religion as a universal obsessional neurosis. The most essential similarity would reside in the underlying renunciation of the activation of instincts that are constitutionally present; and the chief difference would lie in the nature of those instincts, which in the neurosis are exclusively sexual in their origin, while in religion, they spring from egoistic sources. A progressive renunciation of constitutional instincts, whose activation might afford the ego primary pleasure, appears to be one of the foundations of the development of human civilization.
>
> (Freud, 1907: 126)

The crucial connection Freud makes between the individual and the cultural is twofold here. First, we see a mirror-like 'counterpart' to the 'formation of religion' being described, which is 'obsessional neurosis'. The formation of religion is what occurs at the level of culture, and culture itself is for Freud, as we will see, one of the achievements of 'the development of human civilization'. The obsessional-neurotic counterpart to this process is the disorder that occurs at the level of the individual. This then gives us an opening to understand how 'obsessional neurosis' appears as a concomitant of a certain kind of civilization, and so the psychoanalyst is pitched into a series of debates about the nature of our culture today.

The second aspect of the connection between the individual and culture is in the way Freud describes the 'sexual' as operating at the level of the individual and ego as operating at the level of culture. There is an implicit contrast here that can only be grasped if we remember that the 'instincts' that Freud refers to here are actually 'drives' – the word Freud uses in the original German text is 'drive' (*Trieb*), not the German word which refers to hard-wired biological processes – and that 'egoistic' is a rather clumsy translation of what concerns the 'I'. There is a relation between the individual and the cultural here that Freud describes as occurring inside the subject. Our 'individual' as well as the obsessional-neurotic distress that afflicts them is always already cultural. This raises questions about the 'development of human civilization', and what Freud means by 'civilization' as something conceptually distinct from culture.

Civilization

Freud's well-known phrase 'Civilization and Its Discontents', which is taken from the standard translated title of his book of that name, is often read as a diagnosis of the particular forms of Western culture in which psychoanalysis itself took root. It is the kind of civilization that makes us discontented, and that reading of the phrase has led to a rich tradition of political analysis using psychoanalysis. However, while there are certainly aspects of capitalist culture that produce alienation and distress for the individuals who live in it, Freud is actually making a deeper point about the nature of our relations with others. Civilization refers to the particular set of technical accomplishments that we use to define a society, but 'culture' is the underlying stuff of human relatedness that we need as a precondition of any civilization whatsoever. Culture is what the infant enters as they navigate the Oedipus complex as a basic structure of dependency and then autonomy for the individual, and the title of Freud's study is actually 'the uneasiness inherent in culture'. There is no civilization that is not marked by this 'uneasiness', this contradiction between what we desire and those with whom we try to fulfil it:

> In an individual neurosis we take as our starting-point the contrast that distinguishes the patient from his environment, which is assumed to be 'normal'. For a group all of whose members are affected by one and the same disorder no such background could exist; it would have to be found elsewhere. And as regards the therapeutic application of our knowledge, what would be the use of the most correct analysis of social neuroses, since no one possesses authority to impose such a therapy upon the group? But in spite of all these difficulties, we may expect that one day someone will venture to embark upon the pathology of cultural communities.
>
> (Freud, 1930 [1929]: 144)

Again, there is a surprising reversal in Freud's account, a contrast with what we might first expect him to say about normality and abnormality. The 'starting-point' he opens this passage with sets up an opposition between the 'normal' environmental background and the 'disorder' that the individual expresses in the particular form of their distress. Notice that the normal environment and the abnormal 'individual neurosis' are set up here not as absolute properties but as defined in relation to one another.

Then there is the reversal, when Freud points out that one day it may be possible to understand and perhaps provide therapeutic solutions to 'the pathology of cultural communities'. In that case it would be necessary to assume that there was a point from which the analyst could provide the 'correct analysis', and so it would be the individual who was 'normal'. But, as Freud notes, if this were to be possible, then the analyst would not be operating as an individual disconnected from any community, for a 'background' of some kind 'would have to be found elsewhere'. The lesson we can draw from this is that there is no independent point outside culture from which we can give diagnoses of its pathology, and even if one were pushed to imagine such an independent point it would not take the form of an individual.

Analysis

This brings us to one of the most cited and contested phrases in Freud's description of the aims of psychoanalysis as a clinical practice, 'Where id was, there ego shall be.' Once again we should note that the term 'id' gives to the term Freud actually used a specific character that is not there in the original German, which is '*es*' or 'it'. The famous phrase is given a quite specific cultural context in the next clause, when Freud says, 'It is the work of culture – not unlike the draining of the Zuider Zee.' Now, if we follow this metaphor of the 'draining' of the Zuider Zee we can appreciate that this work of analysis, a 'work of culture', involves a 'draining' of the 'it' rather than simply beating it back into the depths of the unconscious. And there is, of course, another aspect of this draining of the Zuider Zee, which is that the land is reclaimed from it so that it is as if we are able to live in the domain of the 'it' rather than being overwhelmed by it. Rather than escaping the 'it', the work of analysis, then, could just as easily be seen as enabling us to inhabit the realm of it:

> . . . certain mystical practices may succeed in upsetting the normal relations between the different regions of the mind, so that, for instance, perception may be able to grasp happenings in the depths of the ego and in the id which were otherwise inaccessible to it. It may be doubted, however, whether this road will lead us to the ultimate truths from which salvation is to be expected. Nevertheless it may be admitted that the therapeutic efforts of psycho-analysis have chosen a similar line of approach. Its intention is, indeed, to strengthen the ego, to make it more independent of the super-ego, to widen its field of perception and enlarge its organization, so that it can appropriate fresh portions of the id. Where id was, there ego shall be. It is the work of culture – not unlike the draining of the Zuider Zee.
>
> (Freud, 1933: 79–80)

Freud argues that we 'appropriate fresh portions' of what has otherwise been inaccessible to us, parts of our lives that have assumed an independent existence and driven us without our conscious assent. He does not argue that we make ourselves independent of those aspects of our existence that have an 'it'-like quality, but he does argue that we can be more independent of the super-ego. We are not being invited to retreat from that which is in us, but to take some distance from what is above us.

Freud is very careful here to limit the claims of psychoanalysis, not to make it seem as if psychoanalysis offers the kind of 'salvation' that 'mystical practices' in religious worldviews have promised in the past. Psychoanalysis does not provide a 'worldview', as we have already pointed out, and so it certainly does not promise 'salvation'. Freud sets up an intriguing contrast here between that road to salvation and ultimate truths and psychoanalysis, and so sets himself against the idea that this is the road that we should travel in order to 'grasp happenings in the depths of the ego and the id which were otherwise inaccessible to it'. The task of psychoanalysis is indeed to widen the 'field of perception' of the 'I', but at the same time to locate that 'I' in culture. Psychoanalysis as a clinical practice is therefore simultaneously a cultural practice, a cultural achievement.

Conclusions

Freud's work has itself turned into a powerful cultural practice, and so we should conclude with some reflections on what we have described and some consequences for the way we might understand the popularity of Freud today.

Every week in newspapers and magazines we find another exposé of Freud as a fraud, and then, in the advice columns and first-person accounts, we read of childhood trauma, repression, denial and the value of talking to someone else about your problems. Rather than treat psychoanalysis simply as a key to unlock the secrets of the subject, psychoanalytic theory should be treated here as a powerful framework because psychoanalytic knowledge helps structure culture.

Freud looked to the collective cultural resources that structure our sense of ourselves and those aspects of our lives that lie outside conscious awareness. Freud invites us to take seriously psychoanalysis as a historically constituted symbolic resource rather than something lying in a mysterious spiritual realm. Such cultural resources do not float beneath the individual unconscious of each of us, but operate as an unconscious cultural precondition for us to think of ourselves as individuals. A multiplicity of tacit understandings, unacknowledged assumptions and unintended consequences frame our lives as we encounter and manage relations with others.

There are many different psychoanalytic resources with competing vocabularies, and so we need to acknowledge that there is no one correct interpretation, or one correct psychoanalytic system for the wording of an interpretation. It is the nature of the unconscious, the unconscious produced for us in culture now, to be riven by contradictory meanings, and the nature of contemporary consciousness is to tolerate these contradictions, and to smooth them over.

Psychoanalysis is a rational therapeutic enterprise, a theoretical framework in the human sciences to notice contradiction. We struggle, then, over the tension between different contradictory understandings. Each version of psychoanalysis has an appeal within specific cultural arenas, and it would be a mistake to propose one version as applicable to all. Different individuals may have recourse to different forms of psychoanalytic argument on different occasions to understand themselves. Even resistance or the attempt to repudiate a certain form of psychoanalysis may be voiced from within a discursive framework that is structured by other different competing psychoanalytic suppositions. For example, someone may declare that they do not like psychoanalysis because it does not take seriously what people say about the reasons they do things, but then the same person may employ the idea that there are things we know about ourselves that are outside immediate awareness.

Different forms of psychoanalysis that are prevalent within contemporary culture are thus collective phenomena, and these collective phenomena will then manifest themselves for each individual subject in the clinic in distinct idiosyncratic ways. The psychoanalyst needs to know something of the forms that psychoanalysis takes in culture, and what the individual brings from culture into the clinic. There is no one specific form of psychoanalysis in culture, rather a competing network of contradictory notions, and a clinician working within a particular theoretical framework will need to know something about the range of psychoanalytic notions that an individual will bring to therapy as their own theoretical frames of self-reference. This kind of psychoanalytic subjectivity is the site upon which psychoanalysis might work, for without such a historically constituted form of subjectivity there will be nothing to engage with, no sense for the analysand that there is something 'unconscious' that is other to themselves, and so nothing for the analyst to interpret.

It is easy to write off psychoanalytic therapy as self-indulgence, and many psychologists spend much energy proving that Freud was 'unscientific' or corrupt, but that is really beside the point. The reason why discussions of Freud and the Freudians seem so interminable and obsessive is that psychoanalysis is so deeply woven into the fabric of our culture. It is there in our gossip about other people's experiences and strange ideas and it is there in our gossip about others and ourselves.

5 Losing psychoanalysis in translation

I chose this chapter title in part to evoke the title of a film, *Lost in Translation* (Coppola, 2003), which was ostensibly about US outsiders coping with being in a place, Japan, which they could not decipher. Actually, the film was not really about being in Japan at all, except insofar as the narrative required that they were somewhere strange; that it was Japan did not figure save as a setting for some jokes about that culture. Instead, the lack of 'translation' in which the characters were lost was the impossible relation between the man and the woman. This question of an 'impossible relation' brings us to psychoanalysis, to the specific tradition in psychoanalysis that I explore in this chapter.

Lacan's work is often thought to be impossible to comprehend partly because his writings and the transcripts of his public seminars are cryptic and convoluted, but also because there is no good translation of his work into English. There is a language barrier between French and English, no doubt about it, but this is nothing to the cultural barriers that there are between different parts of the world that have taken on board psychoanalytic ideas. Previous chapters outlined the way that 'French' psychoanalytic ideas, particularly in Lacan's work, have developed in a quite different direction from the 'US' and 'British' traditions in psychoanalysis (which together comprise a broad and varied 'ego-psychology').

This chapter focuses on and explores consequences of some of the key questions, including 'translation', in Lacan's version of psychoanalysis in relation to the mainstream 'ego-psychology' in the English-speaking world. Here you can see how the reduction of psychoanalytic description to the level of the psychological individual is important not only for psychologists but also for psychosocial researchers studying the clinic as a cultural form.

Translation is one of the battlefields of psychoanalysis; or perhaps it is more accurate to say that there are many battlefields on the terrain that we fight over; one of the latest frontlines is declared to be, in Jacques-Alain Miller's (1998: 141) words, 'the reconquest of the Freudian Field . . . specially in the countries of the English language'. But it is necessary to take stock for a moment and think about what the stakes are in translation, for one of the defining characteristics of language in wars of conquest and reconquest, colonial occupation and national liberation, is that things are not what they seem, and they cannot be made completely visible to both sides.

To abbreviate the argument a little, and to borrow from Lacan's (1975/1988: 12) assertion that 'there's no such thing as a sexual relationship', there's no such thing as a colonial relationship. The drive for clarity by one side, which is usually the colonial power, is often experienced by the other as the imposition of certain sets of meaning, even as the imposition of the idea that in a language there should be certain sets of meaning. On the other side, ambiguous and poetic play of language, which may be part of a strategy of opacity and resistance employed by the oppressed faced with a colonial administration, is often countered by the accusation that these subjects are evasive, and probably untrustworthy (Ashcroft *et al.*, 1995).

Two of the battlefields are worth looking at further. One is the lingering problem of how to translate Freud, and the other is the notion of translation we operate with in clinical work. There is a danger that we move too fast to understand what the problem is in the translation of Freud and use our understanding of that problem as a template to tackle translation in psychoanalytic practice as such. Or, as a kind of compromise formation, there is the temptation to keep those two spheres separate and allow the discussions from each to run in parallel, ensuring that lessons from one never touch or disturb what we are doing in the other. Against these temptations and dangers, I want to draw attention to how our relation to language in clinical work has implications for how we think about what we hope for when we read Freud and, now more to the point, Lacan in English.

Translating Freud

First, let us look briefly at some of the debates over the translation of Freud into English. The proliferation of sensationalized versions of Freud's writings in the early years of the twentieth century led to an attempt to standardize the translation. But *The Standard Edition of the Complete Psychological Works of Sigmund Freud* overseen by James Strachey is, of course, notoriously unreliable. Bruno Bettelheim (1986) tried to put the record straight in his little book *Freud and Man's Soul* shortly before he died, and his aim was twofold: to correct some of the misconceptions about psychoanalysis that had arisen from mistakes in the *Standard Edition* version, and to keep alive some of the lyrical and evocative qualities of Freud's writing.

With respect to the mistakes, Bettelheim pointed out, for example, that the German term *Seele*, which he signals, in the title of his book, as 'Soul', is rendered in English as 'mental apparatus'. This kind of terminology might have served well enough to humour the medics who wanted to persuade their colleagues about the natural scientific credentials of psychoanalysis, but it pressed psychoanalytic practice into something alien to it so that it would not be alien to those who wanted to make it useful in their existing treatments. At the same time, the experiential resonance of Freud's writing was wiped away in the translation of the German terms for 'I', 'Above-I' and 'It' (*Ich*, *Uber-Ich* and *Es*) as ego, super-ego and id.

Eventually, of course, the percolation of psychoanalytic terminology through Western culture meant that many people could feel comfortable enough with talking about their 'ego' and suchlike (Parker, 1997). However, the very success of that new vocabulary is part of the problem, and those who wish to contest the translation now risk being positioned as the revisionists. Some of the grossest mistranslations are readily acknowledged, and the new official translation of the *Standard Edition* overseen by Mark Solms, for example, takes on board some of Bettelheim's arguments – that *Trieb*, for example, should be translated as 'drive' instead of as 'instinct'. The problem is not so much that this type of correction is too little but that the English edition already effectively tidies up and standardizes psychoanalytic concepts not only for the English but even for those now reading Freud in German; the notes in the *Gesammelte Werke* are translations of those written in English for the *Standard Edition*, and thus are framed by the Strachey project of medicalizing and naturalizing psychoanalysis (Timms and Segal, 1998).

Solms (2004) is a neuroscientist, and works closely with researchers like Peter Fonagy and Mary Target (2004), and so the new translation is, again, informed by the agenda to make Freud compatible with a particular version of evidence-based research (Westen *et al.*, 2004). This agenda has been embraced by many in the International Psychoanalytical Association (IPA) – of which Solms and Fonagy are members – in an attempt to solve what the IPA Newsletters repeatedly refer to as '*the crisis in psychoanalysis*'. Science and evidence are closely linked in this agenda, and psychoanalysis that does not meet scientific 'evidence-based' criteria will, it seems, be given up by those researchers if need be (Fonagy, 2000).

The problem, then, is that the ground-rules for what will count as accurate translation already embed what will count within those rules, and give the illusion of clarity. A theory of language as well as of the 'mental apparatus' is presumed, in which signifiers from one language system have equivalents in another; and the expectation is that there can thereby be free circulation of concepts so that psychoanalysis can compete in the therapy market; as if it too was a readily exchangeable commodity to which we could assign a value while we also assign an agreed value to each of its component concepts (Brousse, 2004).

Translation in the clinic

Let us turn to the notion of translation we mobilize in our clinical work, at least if we are Lacanians, and we will see what the stakes are from the other side of the question. I want to address this by looking again at our old friend the 'fresh brains' man discussed by Ernst Kris (1951) in his paper 'Ego psychology and interpretation in psychoanalytic therapy', and digested, regurgitated and digested again by Lacan in different places. The take on Kris I want to focus on is that contained in Lacan's (2006) *Écrits*; it is a reworked and expanded section from *Seminar I*, Lacan's (1956) 'Response to Jean Hyppolite's Commentary on Freud's "*Verneinung*"'.

Kris's paper, originally presented at a 1948 panel on 'technical implications of ego psychology' at the American Psychoanalytic Association, was published in *Psychoanalytic Quarterly* in 1951, preceded by a paper by Rudolph Loewenstein (Lacan's analyst) and followed by one from Heinz Hartmann. So this is a fairly central paper from the trio responsible for the development of ego-psychology. The 'progressive integration' of hypotheses in psychoanalysis based on the 'development of the structural point of view' in Freud's work links two notions of development: that of the discipline of psychoanalysis and that of the individual analysand. The treatment then works backwards from what we now understand Freud to be aiming towards: 'His [Freud's] advice that analysis should start from the surface, and that resistance be analyzed before interpreting content implies principles basic in ego psychology' (Kris, 1951: 16).

Kris a couple of times in the paper actually pulls back from an endorsement of the view that analysis should proceed through 'layers'. (This was an argument that had been most forcefully advocated by Wilhelm Reich, and in particular Reich's (1972) work on 'character analysis' first published in 1945 was, despite his expulsion from the IPA in 1934, still discussed in psychoanalytic training at the time Kris was writing.) However, there is an assumption that psychoanalytic practice should be based on 'a correct knowledge of the infantile pattern' (Kris, 1951: 24), and that then it will be possible to engage in 'planning and predicting' interventions (ibid.: 26); there is thus a conception of 'normal progress' in the sequences of interpretation and resistance by the analysand (ibid.: 21). It is that end point in the chain of faulty connections in the developmental story of ego-psychology, where it deals with the phenomenon of 'resistance' that Lacan is primarily concerned with in his commentary on Kris. Lacan's expanded commentary here (after his 'excommunication' from the IPA) differs significantly from his discussion of the case in 1954 (when efforts were still being made to repair the unexpected problems that arose from the formation of the Société Française de Psychanalyse): Lacan does not refer to the response of Kris's patient as 'acting out' after a bad interpretation, and is more concerned with how Kris conceptualizes his own 'alleged interpretation of the surface'; if anything, Lacan's (1975/1991: 60) characterization of Kris's intervention (and remember, Hartmann was then IPA President) is glowing with praise: 'Here you can see what makes for a response elicited by accurate interpretation, namely a level of speech which is both paradoxical and full in its meaning.' The occasion is, as the title of Lacan's commentary indicates, a response to a reading of Freud's paper on 'negation' in which 'resistance' figures as a key motif. Freud (1925: 239) concludes his discussion with the assertion, rehearsed at the beginning of the paper, that 'There is no stronger evidence that we have been successful in our efforts to uncover the unconscious than when the patient reacts to it with the words "I didn't think that", or "I didn't (ever) think of that".'

Kris locates 'resistance' on the side of the analysand, and so his aim is to understand and interpret defences so that the real meaning of his analysand's behaviour can be made as clear to the analysand as it is to the analyst. The 'patient', as we will refer to him (following Kris), is a scientist in his early thirties who had already been in analysis, with Melitta Schmideberg (Melanie Klein's daughter) – for an account of this 'first analysis' see Schmideberg (1938) – and so this second analysis also serves to illustrate how advances in ego-psychology that provide interpretations 'closer to the surface' can go further than the albeit 'considerable improvement' achieved so far (Kris, 1951: 21); the set of interpretations provided in the second analysis, Kris says, 'covered a large number of details of behaviour and therefore opened the way to linking present and past, adult symptomatology and infantile fantasy', and the key was 'exploration of the surface' (ibid.: 24).

The patient sought the second analysis with Kris due to an inhibition about publication. Kris says that the patient was 'anxious that his resumption of analysis should not come to the notice of his previous analyst' and was convinced that 'he should now be analyzed by a man' (ibid.: 22). There are a host of other issues in this case – including the position of Kris in the transference as a 'subject supposed to know' that should then be the site of a knowledge that the patient may have been anxious to plagiarize – that we do not have space to cover here. The patient felt unable to publish his research because he felt 'under constant pressure of an impulse to use somebody else's ideas' (ibid.: 22). His father had not matched up to the achievements of his grandfather, and so, Kris argues, the 'projection of ideas to paternal figures was in part determined by the wish for a great and successful father' (a 'grand' father) (ibid.: 23); the 'behavior pattern' Kris was discovering through the patient's life was a 'tendency to take, to bite, to steal', and this tendency was eventually displaced to 'ideas' (ibid.).

Kris describes how the patient turned up to one particular session after having found a 'treatise' in a library that contained the very ideas he was working on, and he reported this to his analyst in a 'paradoxical tone of satisfaction and excitement' (ibid.: 22). Kris claims that 'extended scrutiny' of this supposition revealed that the treatise contained no such ideas, and that the patient had instead 'made the author [of the treatise] say what he wanted to say himself'. The passage Lacan quotes from Kris's paper runs as follows:

> Only the ideas of others were truly interesting, only ideas one could take; hence the taking had to be engineered. At this point of the interpretation I was waiting for the patient's reaction. The patient was silent and the very length of the silence had a special significance. Then, as if reporting a sudden insight, he said 'every noon, when I leave here, before luncheon, and before returning to my office, I walk through X Street (a street well known for its small but attractive restaurants) and I look at the menus in the windows. In one of the restaurants I usually find my preferred dish – fresh brains'.
>
> (Kris, 1951: 23, cited in Lacan, 1956: 331)

Now, there are two aspects of Lacan's scathing comments on this account that we should notice. The first concerns the way that Kris falls into line with the patient's declared concern that he is plagiarizing the ideas of others, and Kris reinforces the very notions of 'plagiarism' and 'intellectual property' by leading his patient to the conclusion that this was not really the case. However, the issue for Kris was that the patient thought he was a plagiarist; the patient thus 'engineered' things so that the ideas he would take would be the ideas of others. Because 'extended scrutiny' convinces the analyst that he knows what the reality of the situation is – that his patient is not a plagiarist – he thinks he can then use his understanding of that reality as a ground from which to help the patient understand that he 'engineered' the plagiarism so that he can take (take ideas, for instance) from others. This kind of interpretation therefore relies on also reassuring the patient that the analyst, and then both analyst and patient, can be clear about what reality is.

Against this kind of interpretation, Lacan (1956: 329) points out that 'we should not assure someone that he is not in the least bit guilty because he accuses himself of bad intentions'. While Kris seems very content with his patient's reaction to his interpretation, Lacan interprets it as a case of 'acting out'; the analyst's crass interpretations lead the patient to tell his analyst of his search outside the analysis for 'fresh brains'.

Resistance to translation

Freud (1900/1999: 336) commented, in *The Interpretation of Dreams*, that 'whatever disturbs the continuation of the work of analysis is resistance'. But we need to comprehend how resistance is structured in the analytic setting, and one way to do that is to attend to the lure of understanding, the lure of wanting to translate what the patient says into what the analyst can understand. As Lacan pointed out, this is a question not so much to do with what lies inside the mind of the patient as how the discourse, the arrangement of signifiers in the analytic meeting is structured. This is one reason why it is preferable, Lacan (1964/1973: 68) says, to speak of 'resistance of discourse, when the discourse proceeds towards the condensation around the nucleus' of a trauma, than to speak of 'resistance of the subject' which implies a pre-existing self-sufficient ego responsible for psychic phenomena.

When there is a blockage, a slippage or a silence in the analysand's speech we might guess that this resistance is because the analysand is thinking about the analyst. Resistance is here a sign of transference, appearing for the analysand on the side of the analyst. So we can read Lacan's argument that 'resistance is on the side of the analyst' as a translation, or rather a deliberate mistranslation of the notion of 'counter-transference'. Lacan's strategy here entails, we might say, a resistance to translation to conceptualize and tackle resistance. It is, at least, a way of addressing and reframing what therapists who talk about 'counter-transference' are concerned about (Burgoyne and Sullivan, 1997). Lacan's argument is sometimes formulated even more strongly as 'there is no other resistance to analysis than that of the analyst' (Lacan, 1958: 497).

The 'resistance' that is attributed to the patient is actually a function of the way the analyst sets up the task of treating the patient as a text which he, the analyst, must render legible. The outcome, Lacan (1958: 331) points out, is that 'the analysis of the subject's behaviour patterns amounts to inscribing his behaviour in the analyst's patterns'. We can thus read Lacan's argument against ego-psychology as an argument against a particular notion of 'translation' in clinical practice; Lacan comments that the principles that are at work in Kris's paper are 'the appeal to the subject's ego, the approach "from the surface," the reference to reality' (Lacan 1958: 328).

The second aspect of Lacan's sarcastic commentary (one that repeats the response the patient delivers to Kris) is a critique of Kris that is embedded in another critique, of the way that Kris has translated psychoanalytic clinical practice into a hostile culture and a vocabulary that is antithetical to psychoanalysis. We know very well how Lacan hated the 'New Deal of ego psychology' (ibid.), but we have a specific closely textured example in the Kris case of how the notions of 'intellectual property' that the analyst buys into are part of what Lacan calls the 'success-oriented context of American culture' (ibid.: 329).

When Lacan retains the term 'New Deal' in English it is to draw attention to the peculiar nature of that culture; all the more so when he preserves the English for 'scholar', 'success' and 'patterns'; and all the more pointedly when he asks if Kris believes that his intervention has enabled the patient to find 'a valid way out of this id' – and pointing out in a footnote that 'id' is 'the standard English translation of Freud's *Es*' (Lacan, 1956: 333). Lacan here is keeping open a critical distance from the English terminology, maintaining a space against the 'translation' of these concepts from one language system into the other.

Translating Lacan

Too many of the disputes about the translation of Lacan into English are now governed by theoretical coordinates that insidiously translate psychoanalysis into something else. This is despite the translators themselves often warning us that we should not trust them to produce something crystal clear (Fink, 2004a).

Bruce Fink's new translation of the complete *Écrits* (Lacan, 2006) has been accompanied by some useful reflections on the process of translation. His book *Lacan to the Letter: Reading* Écrits *Closely* (Fink, 2004b), for example, brings together essays that unravel some of the complexities of the text and serve to rebut critics – like Sokal and Bricmont (1998), for example – who read Lacan too fast so that his work can then be easily dismissed for not chiming with common sense or with science reduced to a form of common sense (Fink, 2004b). It is worth noting, incidentally, that for US pragmatists the meaningful and technical aspects of knowledge are closely bound together. Because they are concerned with what works, psychoanalytic writing that challenges what we take for granted, that defies public understanding, that refuses to function as a toolbox, and that also defies scientists' attempts to be useful, must be seen by pragmatists as doubly problematic (Glynos and Stavrakakis, 2002).

This US pragmatist tradition, and the particular kind of conceptual grid it imposes on psychoanalysis as it comprehends, absorbs and neutralizes it, is subtly different from the English empiricist tradition. Empiricists base knowledge on experience, and there is an emphasis on phenomena that can be observed; there is the presumption that objects of study must be conceptually and actually self-identical, and one consequence is that this tradition is more concerned with limits to what is possible. The moral lesson of this tradition is that when you know what the world is like you should then give up trying to change it. The pragmatists, on the other hand, are so keen to adapt people to society precisely because they believe that anything is possible; this is one reason why they just do not get Lacan's complaint about adaptation and ego-psychology.

Lacan (1961–1962) spends some time addressing the necessary illusion of self-identity in *Seminar IX* as a prelude to his elaboration of the differential quality of the signifier and the function of the unary trait. Again and again Lacan opposes developmentalist versions of psychoanalysis that pretend that it is possible to actually observe patterns of interaction between an infant and its mother and so ground normal and pathological processes in linear causal processes occurring in real time. Such experimental studies have, nevertheless, proceeded apace in the United States, in the work of Daniel Stern (1985), and they have been eagerly seized upon by the British tradition in psychoanalysis, one that has always included 'child observation' in its training (Miller *et al.*, 1989; Burman, 1997). There is, of course, a fateful collusion between pragmatism and empiricism today in the rise of 'evidence-based' medicine which warrants, among other things, the spread of cognitive behavioural therapy from the United States to Europe.

Fink also points out, in an article on translating Lacan, for the *Journal for Lacanian Studies*, that 'we are surrounded by miserable translations of French texts' (Fink, 2004a). He includes some astounding examples from Sheridan's version of the selection from the *Écrits* (Lacan, 1977), and then some amusing examples from his own mistranslations so we can be sure that we do not leave with the message that Fink will sort it all out for us.

More fresh brains

To return to the 'fresh brains' man for a moment, there are aspects of Fink's own commentary in the footnotes that are quite intriguing. Notwithstanding the insinuations Lacan makes in the course of his commentary, it does not seem as if Kris explicitly reassured his patient. The assurance, though, creeps into the 'understanding' that Kris claims to have about the reality of the situation. Kris certainly does not say, as Lacan (2006: 329) claims, that he asked 'to see the book from the library [and then] reads it'. There are other moments in Lacan's account where he misrepresents what Kris says and exaggerates for effect, to make a point about the logic of ego-psychological technique. For example, Lacan (2006: 329) says that the patient arrived at the session Kris describes after having 'merely glanced' at the treatise in the library 'some time ago', whereas in fact Kris (1951: 22) says that 'It was a treatise with which he had been familiar, since he had glanced at it some time ago.' That is, Kris does already characterize the error of attribution as more credible, and Lacan errs on the side of scepticism about the claims the analysand might make.

When Kris, at the beginning of the little extract from his paper that Lacan quotes, and that we have included here, says that because, for the patient, '[o]nly the ideas of others were truly interesting, only ideas one could take; hence the taking had to be engineered' (Kris, 1951: 23, cited in Lacan, 2006: 331), it is possible to read this a little more generously than Lacan did. It is possible to read this aspect of the interpretation as itself a critical comment on the kind of culture in which, as Lacan (2006: 329) puts it; 'the impact of the inhibition on his vocation' should loom so large. Perhaps Kris was as queasy as Lacan about the American way of life; and the difference between them here was not so much that one was there, and adapted to it, and the other was not, and able to disdain it more easily, but that Kris should still, by way of his comment, have introduced into the analytic session an element of reality testing and judgement about the particular nature of the symbolic system that he, Kris, could see, and the patient could not. Would Lacan have done otherwise?

Fink's gloss on this, on the other hand, is perhaps a little too generous, if not to Kris, then to the symbolic system he then had to inhabit and work through with his patient. Fink at least (and it is a measure of how valuable this translation of the *Écrits* is that Fink makes decisions about translation visible) tell us that he has omitted something from the text: it is Lacan's comment on the English term 'engineering' that suggests that it is 'related to the famous American "how to," or, if not, to the notion of planning (discussed in the last section of Kris' article)' (Fink, 'Translator's Endnotes', in Lacan, 2006: 798). It seems to me, from the standpoint of someone outside US culture, that this connection between 'engineering' and 'planning' is quite plausible (even if Kris himself did not personally subscribe to it).

Lacan smuggles some theoretical concepts into his own translation of the extracts from Kris's paper into French, which Fink then spots as contraband

and so does not let through into English. But these – Lacan's – illicit additions to the text actually also enrich it. For example, Fink complains that Lacan renders 'attractive restaurants' as 'attentive restaurants', and Fink comments that 'Lacan perhaps confuses "attractive" with "attentive" here, because he suggests that these are restaurants where one is well looked after, or well attended to' (ibid.). It would be possible to read this as Lacan introducing the idea that desire for the Other is also desire of the Other; it is attractive to be attended to by those who are attractive to the subject.

This raises another problem with the 'translation' from one language into another. In his 'translator's note' to the English edition of *Seminar I*, John Forrester (in Lacan, 1975/1991: vii) states that he has 'aimed at an exact translation'; nevertheless, he immediately acknowledges that 'this involves, however, finding appropriate colloquial English to correspond to a text that is both informal and complex'. Only by navigating a line between 'exact translation' and 'colloquial English' will it be possible to arrive at something 'corresponding as faithfully as possible with the original text' (ibid.). It is sometimes said that the United States and Britain are divided by a common language, and Fink includes colloquial English that jars on the English ear ('pinkies' and suchlike). The translation of Lacan into US American English also gives rise to a Fink (1997) version of psychoanalysis that has already unwittingly injected cultural presuppositions into it (Parker, 1999b). It is some comfort that this division within language is compatible with Lacan's theory of the signifier as already a point of division at the very moment it appears to be singular and unitary (Lacan, 1961–1962).

On the other side, the French side of the language barrier, there is also some uncertainty about what it is we are translating *from*. We do not really know what the 'original text' is in the first place. Cormac Gallagher (2005: 7) points out, with respect to Fink's translation of *Seminar XX*, that the 'official Miller version from which he was working had seriously distorted the spoken word in such a way as to seriously obscure the specifically new steps that Lacan was taking that year'. There is a tidying up of the text that has already started before the translation into English, and this interference (if this is how we should view it) is warranted by Miller in his assertion in the 'Editor's Note' for *Seminar XI* that this would be 'an authentic version that would stand, in the future, for the original, which does not exist' (Miller, 'Editor's Note' in Lacan, 1964/1973, also cited by Gallagher, 2005: 5). The rage at the Miller control of the text as an 'established', for Gallagher (2005: 6) 'Maoist', text is palpable and understandable; but the argument that we should give up the illusion that we could retrieve the original text is still surely one that we should take seriously.

Jean Hyppolite's commentary on Freud's text *Negation*, to which Lacan's little excursus on Kris is a response, points out that the 'explicit symbol [of negation] alone makes possible something like the use of the unconscious, all the while maintaining the repression' (Hyppolite, 1956: 753); there is, in Hyppolite's commentary a reading of Freud as outlining a theory of repression that does not so much press down on something that already exists but which constitutes that which it operates upon. In Freud's (1925: 237) own text we find him reminding the reader that 'all presentations originate from perceptions and are repetitions of them'. This leads us to a very different notion of 'reality testing' than the ego-psychology version excoriated by Lacan in his reading of Kris. For Freud, and Lacan, the aim of reality testing is 'not to find an object in real perception which corresponds to the one presented, but to refind an object, to convince oneself that it is still there' (Freud, 1925: 237–238).

Perhaps the closest Lacan came to an account of the impossibility of translating from one language to another, I suggest, was in his account of sexual difference. The relation between languages is factored differently at different points in history, and I do not want to essentialize the nature of French as the language from which we translate Lacan and English as the language in which these debates about translation are taking place. Nevertheless, it might be worth reflecting on the way that the process of learning the French language poses particular problems for boys in English schools. It is often commented upon, for example, that the speaking of French with the correct accent is threatening to English boys because it seems feminine and feminizing. Perhaps it feels closer, in fact, to what Lacan (1975/1991: 55) referred to as the 'affective smoochy-woochy' of the therapists against which his analysis was pitted, and there would indeed be an irony if this was the case.

The resistance to French might then be handled in such a way as to keep the repression of Lacan in place, precisely by the endeavour of insisting on the translation of the slippery, feminine French into clear, masculine English. That is, the insistence on clear translation could be something pathetically phallic, and doomed to fail. Against this, attending to the necessary disjunction between languages, and perhaps also then to the antagonism between different forms of psychoanalysis in different cultures, would, instead, keep open a space for psychoanalysis as such against the illusion of translation.

As Lacan (1975/1991: 261) insisted in *Seminar I*, 'truth emerges from a mistake', but we need to keep open the space for the mistake so that truth can appear. If we close it up, and try to avoid the mistakes, then there will be no yield of truth. The point I am making is perhaps a very trivial one, but I am concerned with what happens if we lose sight of it when we read about the difficulty of translating Lacan into English and we are led to think that those difficulties can be solved.

Conclusions

It may be a sign of the changing relationship to language in psychoanalysis, in different forms of psychoanalysis, that the various traditions in the International Psychoanalytical Association are now so firmly implanted in the English language that we – and I speak from the vantage point of the English speakers, of course, for this is our problem – know the terms of the debates so well that we feel comfortable in the threads of the discourse. Gone are the days when thickly accented middle-Europeans would provide the caricature psychoanalytic figures much beloved by Hollywood films, and gone are the attempts to puzzle over what they are actually talking about. Instead, the illusion of perfect translation has come to be but one aspect of the sedimentation of IPA traditions of analysis in English-speaking common sense. One of the consequences of that sedimentation, of course, is that it is then likely to end up not being psychoanalysis at all.

The instances when a psychoanalyst from outside the English language gets an icy reception from IPA types expecting clarity of exposition are symptomatic. There is the painful example of Lacan speaking in London to members of the British Psychoanalytical Society in 1963 and losing the word in English, appropriately enough, for *reste*, the remainder that he was at that point elaborating as *objet petit a* (in Roudinesco, 1990: 350). (Notice that we retain the French terminology for this object so that it can be transmitted better by way of the algorithms that comprise Lacanian psychoanalysis, notwithstanding the 'frequent anomalies' that result according to Gallagher, 2005: 15.) His audience watched him struggle, and one can imagine their satisfaction at being able simultaneously to confirm that this man was speaking nonsense and that nonsense is not what they want to find in psychoanalysis.

Against this manifestation of adaptation of psychoanalysis to the English language is another aspect of the changing relationship in different traditions; that is, that Lacanians here – if you will forgive me for marking 'here' as English space; and there is a debate to be had about how this is and how it can change – do still face that feeling of incomprehension when our learned colleagues from France, for example, come here to speak to us. They are coming into English, as Jacques-Alain Miller (1998: 141) puts it, to 'quit the enclosure of the Latins', and we must struggle to make sense of what is going on and struggle every time with the experience that we cannot exactly make sense of what is going on. A whole session in London with a speaker from Paris, for example, was devoted to 'ciphering' and deciphering of *jouissance* in the body and so on, and a question came from the floor at the end which indicated that the word 'ciphering' had been interpreted all the way through the session as 'shivering', and why not?

This productive nonsense is only possible if we refuse the idea that everything in psychoanalysis can be perfectly translated from one language to another; this is a process of 'reducing the signifiers into their nonsensicality' (in a modified translation by Nobus and Quinn (2005: 189) of the Alan Sheridan translation of Lacan (1964/1973) which is 'reducing the non-meaning of the signifiers'), one that opens up an attention to history rather than sealing over what has happened in the history that has made psychoanalysis possible. The phenomenon of being 'outside' thus marks the enduring quality of the lack of closure of human experience that psychoanalysis brings us face to face with.

This is something that the search for accurate translation of Lacan into English could cover over, and the problem is that while this would be a very English thing to do, it would be the antithesis of psychoanalysis; then we would indeed be lost.

6 Marxism, psychoanalysis and the state

Lessons from Slovenia

This chapter explores cultural-political interventions and the role of different practical-theoretical perspectives on the state, on the nature of the state and on strategies to tackle it. It thus raises questions for the field of psychosocial studies which has the ambition of being 'critical', for surely critique should be as much about political structures that condition our work as about concepts and methods in the discipline of psychology. Framing of the task in terms of dismantling, negotiating or subverting the state already, of course, highlights differences of analytic and political strategy.

I am concerned here with the relationship between Marxism and psychoanalysis and the ways that differences between the two traditions of work play out in actual political interventions. The contradictory elements of Marxism and psychoanalysis can be conceptually organized through this mapping, in which it will also be possible to determine their relationship with capitalism and forms of bureaucratic state management.

So Marxism is the main reference point for organizing this discussion, and psychoanalysis is here articulated as a practice in relation to it. Psychoanalysis is sometimes associated in academic debate with Marxist perspectives – and many debates in psychosocial studies are informed to some extent by implicitly Marxist assumptions about the nature of ideology and consciousness – but psychoanalytic clinical practice does not have the same immediate relation to the state. Even though it has always had to operate within the constraints of specific state practices, psychoanalysts have often been able to pretend that they are merely concerned with personal change, and that this can proceed independently of political activity. As you will see, the 'lessons from Slovenia' that I refer to come from the political practice of a cultural-political movement, NSK, that mobilizes ideas from both psychoanalysis and Marxism while disturbing the way we usually understand those theoretical frameworks.

The cultural-political movement I will describe operates, for specific geographical and historical reasons, in a peculiar space between Marxism and psychoanalysis. This movement, NSK, developed in Slovenia in the 1980s as the Yugoslav state began to disintegrate, and it then developed distinctive strategies to question the role of the state as it operated until 1990 and the new independent state that was formed in 1991. Elements of this cultural practice, specifically 'overidentification', have been described by Slavoj Žižek (1989) and this is a motif that runs from his early to recent political writings.

Because the Socialist Federal Republic of Yugoslavia claimed allegiance to Marxism, even to a form of open socialist self-management, the particular psychoanalytic theoretical resources that were accumulated by the opposition in Slovenia were already positioned in relation to Marxism, and in practice in opposition to an actually existing socialist state. But before we can explore that ambiguous position, and how NSK set about conceptualizing and subverting it, it is necessary to clarify that which Marxism was formed to combat and replace: capitalism.

Capitalism

Capitalism can be characterized, from the standpoint of Marxism, in the broadest, most open sense of the revolutionary Marxist tradition, in the following way (Bensaïd, 2002).

Capitalism, first, is a political economic system in which there is *exploitation* of the labouring classes. This exploitation requires control, if not now always immediate ownership, of the means of production that is organized around profit obtained from surplus value produced by workers. It requires, second, that the relationship between capitalist and worker be treated as something that is permanent and unchanging. The relationship is thus essentialized, though this *essentialism* may be ideologically justified either as the kind of relationship necessary to civilized society or as expressing the natural tendencies of human beings to compete for resources and sell their labour to others. Third, capitalism rests on a particular conception of individual *rights*: the rights of those who own the means of production to employ others for profit, and of course the rights of workers to sell their labour power and to view that exchange as if it formed a contract that was consciously and freely one that both parties engaged in.

There is, fourth, an enclosure of natural resources so that these resources can then be bought and sold, and so that it is necessary for those who engaged in subsistence farming as part of a peasant economy to choose to instead become part of the industrial workforce. This commodification of natural resources has a logic in which there must be a governance of *territoriality* as the market economy expands, and then there is mutation of the management of territory as finance capital predominates and as various competing forms of imperialist control of foreign land, labour and markets. A fifth point, which runs alongside the essentializing of relationships, is that under capitalism economic relationships are ratified anew in the face of disparate ideological and moral challenges. This *ratification* elaborates the ideological horizon within which capitalism is questioned, this in such a way that there is sedimentation of taken-for-granted ground-rules for production and relationships, ground-rules that are not immediately open to question. Sixth, development of production is viewed as a linear unfolding process, as a given law of economic progress. This apparent *linearity* of capitalist development, and of the natural development of capitalism out of earlier modes of production, is replicated conceptually in causal descriptions of natural and social processes and in the temporal ordering of the working day and of an individual's lifespan. There is a requirement, seventh, that there be a degree of *regulation* by the state of economic relationships, regulation that now operates in conditions of neoliberalism alongside deregulation and the privatization of social welfare services. Capitalism constructs and warrants itself ideologically around the motif of the 'free market', yet the state has always been a necessary regulatory apparatus to ensure that there is 'competition' as well, ensuring that resistance to capitalism is quashed.

Eighth, decisions taken by the exploited to sell their labour power, as well as decisions of the exploiters to invest, are treated as individual decisions, and this *individuality* is often invoked by supporters as a defining principle of capitalist society. There is a corresponding and necessary individualization of the domain of subjective experience so that even attempts to make capitalism run smoothly are viewed as 'state interference'. Ninth, the *rationality* of the system is underpinned by a particular scientistic view of social and personal enlightenment. This ideological armature of science under capitalism is then set against alternative systems, which are derogated as pre-scientific, uncivilized and 'irrational', or may be romanticized as non-rational and intuitive, but usually in such a way as to prioritize the rationality assumed by each individual seeking further enlightenment from them. Finally, the tenth point, there is apparent transparency of social relationships, but this ideological trope of transparency itself functions to intensify the *alienation* suffered under capitalism. This alienation, and the individualizing descriptions and explanations of it, serves to obscure the conditions of life which separates each individual from their creative work.

Analysis

The characteristics of capitalism outlined so far raise a question about the governance of individuality, and the way each individual buys into this economic system or refuses this economic system in such a way as to remain trapped within it. Psychoanalysis is a practice which has often historically been assumed to be of the Left, or is assumed even by many Marxists to provide an implicit if not explicit critique of bourgeois subjectivity (Parker, 2007b). However, it does seem as if, as a clinical practice, psychoanalysis is often actually complicit with capitalist production. The collusion of psychoanalysis with capitalism – even if ambivalently, reluctantly, unwillingly so – is apparent in the following respects. Here we can show how psychoanalysis is mapped into capitalism, which is the mode of production in which it emerged and flourished. I am concerned here with methodological principles of psychoanalysis as an actually existing practice against which certain schools of psychoanalysis define themselves but which still governs the logic of their practice.

The key clinical device of *transference* in psychoanalytic work – the re-enactment of the past of the analysand in the present in relation to the figure of the analyst – requires a conceptual apparatus of ownership and self-management. It also, of course, operates within discrete privatized financial arrangements in which the analysand must pay the analyst, and transference therefore entails the reproduction of relations of power, relations in which the subject has been constituted. Even if there is also the claim that they thereby 'work through' those relations, the analytic process as such is not usually put into question at the end of analysis; 'transference' may then even be assumed by the analysand to operate outside the clinic, which itself is already a popular mistake made by those inducted into psychoanalytic culture. The analysand thus constructs a personal ideological device for experiencing and explaining what exploitation is. Most forms of psychoanalysis aim to reinforce some form of *identity*, though there is some queasiness now about Freud's recommendation that the domain of the ego be enlarged. Some traditions are suspicious of the ego as the central organizing instance, but then there is often a risk that the 'subject' as such, even if conceptualized as a necessarily 'divided subject', is treated as the unit of treatment, and some form of identity is thereby smuggled in by the back door (or a kind of trapdoor leading to the unconscious). If relationships and sedimented individual identities and their component parts are not explicitly essentialized, acceptance of the law, which always also pertains to identity, is effectively reinforced. The rights of each individual are limited conceptually and clinically by an elusive domain of the subject, the unconscious, and this domain remains for ever out of reach. This is all the more so in the ostensibly more radical forms of psychoanalysis which do not pretend to harmonize the relationship between consciousness and the unconscious. Psychic *structure* that governs the particular relationship between conscious complaint and the unconscious is divined by the analyst, who then determines the direction of the treatment and locks each category of subject in its rightful place. The rights of each individual to sell their labour power are questioned but then endorsed within the structure of the clinical treatment, which only begins when there has been a demand for analysis.

Psychoanalysis, in different ways in different theoretical traditions, revolves around the problematic of the *integrity* of the subject. This problematic is not neatly solved in any tradition of psychoanalysis, but reappears through discussions of the nature of the ego as a 'bodily ego', of the nature of 'skin' as a surface of demarcation, of the 'I' who comes to be where 'it' was, of the 'subjectivizing' of the subject, and of the value accorded to 'responsibility' even if conceptualized as being capable of giving response to, accounting. The territory of the individual thus complements the territory of the state as a place from which commerce with others might take place.

There is the assumption that the trajectory of each subject is the product of particular *determination*, and sometimes, it is said, overdetermination by familial relationships or chains of signifiers. These ground-rules are, of course, thrown into question in analysis, but there is very rarely the promise that the analysand will escape such determinations, merely the option of reducing them to nonsense in the analysis and forging a different relationship with them in waking life. Psychoanalysis thus insidiously ratifies the social forces it explores, and the analytic process can often end in a blend of stoicism and cynicism in the face of an outer world that must remain the same.

There is often a causal developmental sequence identified, a *temporality* that has been buttressed by psychoanalytic appeals to evidence from developmental psychology. This temporal relationship is sometimes conceptually reworked in analyses of the production of cause through deferred action by which certain events only become traumatic after the event. This merely serves to enclose the history of the individual subject within a narrative that is more efficiently stitched in place by threads that loop back and make the present into something that will always have been the case. Even the most reflexive histories of capitalism use the same kind of device, to find in its origins what it will become so that economic history is caught in a closed circuit. Most versions of psychoanalysis enable the individual to function in particular societal conditions, even if the psychoanalyst does not actually bring about such *adaptation*. Adaptation to life conditions sometimes proceeds through the path of subversion of identification and ideals, but this then leads to the giving up of political ideals, the idea that another world is possible, to living with and perhaps enjoying the symptom and an acceptance of 'lack'. Like the economic system that houses it, psychoanalysis recognizes that the most adaptable processes are those that are able to work with rather than against innovation.

The particularity of each subject is often reduced to the function of individual characteristics. Above and beyond the claim that a 'clinical case' cannot and should not be applied as a grid to other cases, the *individuality* of a path through analysis is also reproduced in the insistence that the treatment, and even political judgement internal to the school, takes place 'one by one'. Collective processes are viewed as pathological, and ideological warnings about crowds are reproduced in the covertly individualized varieties of group analysis which are factored either as 'ego training in action' or as the treatment of the group as a many-headed individual. Psychoanalysis usually, despite Freud's own warnings, adheres to a distinctive worldview which it assumes to be true, and which is sometimes buoyed up by appeals to science, to scientific method or in claims to be addressing the subject of science. These forms of *truth* are sometimes given a publicly accountable frame, in which case there is an adherence to scientific standards and explicit rationalism. This rationalist truth is then sometimes given a hermetic cast in which its internal logic is even more rigorous than that of mainstream science. Finally, psychoanalysis aims to enable the subject to understand that there is no escape from alienation, and in some versions of psychoanalysis this alienation is viewed as a condition for being a subject, a subject of language. Claims to freedom have always been treated with suspicion in the psychoanalytic tradition, as forms of illusion or delusion. It is, instead, necessary that there be forms of *defence* against the temptation to abolish the social constraints that make us human, and psychoanalysis itself thus functions as a form of defence. It is one of the defence mechanisms capitalism utilizes to warn those who rail against alienation that they will most likely end up with something worse. There is thus a tense, sometimes uneasy, but mainly compliant relationship between psychoanalysis and capitalism.

Marxism

So, what then, of Marxism, and how might Marxism be articulated in relation to capitalism? I have already said that my characterization of capitalism is from the standpoint of Marxism, or rather as an articulation of the standpoint of the working class, which is what Marxism is. We are concerned with the actual material practice of Marxism (just as we have been concerned with the actual material practice of psychoanalysis) rather than with an idealized abstraction or academic social critique. So, we do need to articulate Marxism with how it has actually manifested itself historically under Stalinism, in the so-called 'socialist states' and in the communist parties loyal to those states (Mandel, 1978). This material practice will, of course, be crucial when we come to look at NSK, and so I include here some attention to Stalinism as the political context against which NSK developed. There are also some homologies between the mutation of Marxism into Stalinism and the institutional history of psychoanalysis which are reactivated and subverted in some of the uses that NSK makes of psychoanalysis.

First, Marxism aims for the expansion of *democracy*, up against the limits of capitalist exploitation and then through a necessary break from those limits in a proletarian revolution. This democracy is defined by self-determination by associated producers of the organization and distribution of natural and creative resources. This promise is betrayed by Stalinism: democratic centralism inside the workers' movement is replaced by *centralization* of decision-making and prohibition of opposition in the rest of society. Second, there is an ethos of *change*, in which understanding the world necessarily entails changing it. This refusal of any essentialism is underpinned by a dialectical mode of interrogation of reality which attends to and simultaneously facilitates transformations of social relations. This ontological commitment – to dialectical movement rather than to discrete essences – is replaced as the Stalinist *bureaucracy* crystallizes. Relations become fixed in place, often with an appeal to identity categories such as 'the proletariat' and its leadership. In Marxism, third, self-determination of associated producers reworks notions of *autonomy* so that human rights become defined in relation to freedom understood relationally in an ethical relation to creative labour. This ethical self-transformative capacity is betrayed by pragmatic strategic defence of the bureaucracy in which even opposition to capitalism is instrumentalized. Stalinist *instrumentality* turns political struggle into a tool of the pragmatic needs of the bureaucracy.

Fourth, Marxism is a form of *internationalism*. It is a self-consciously internationalist movement which pits itself against the imperialist and global ambitions of capital to segregate the workforce. Against this, Stalinism revived *nationalism* through the motif of 'socialism in one country' and an appeal to national sentiment in each country where a variety of home-grown bureaucracy ruled. Fifth, Marxism not only restores *meaning* to creative labour but also provides a meaning to the development of capitalism, and then to the forms by which it may be transcended. Stalinism responds with simple appeals to authority and the closing of debates around the interpretation of history around one correct account. This *totalization* also serves, of course, to ratify the power of the bureaucracy as the interpretative tool through which historical determination can be judged and measured. The historical narrative Marxism provides is, sixth, one that learns from the past so as not to repeat it and provides a means by which past struggles against exploitation find redemption. Marxist *history* is therefore also historical intervention in which combined and uneven development is characterized by unexpected connections and leaps which bring history alive again in the revolutionary process. This conception of history is betrayed by Stalinism, which must rewrite the past in order to favour the standpoint of the leadership. This *fixity* of sequence replicates the fixed position of the bureaucracy, and it serves to justify alliances with the 'progressive bourgeoisie' of capitalist economies friendly to the leadership. It serves to fix the narrative into ineluctable sequences of stages of development so that they culminate in present-day arrangements. Seventh, Marxism enables and requires collective *resistance* to capitalism, and resistance to the strategies of divide and rule by which opposition to capitalism is rendered into individual, ethnic or nationalist complaint. Stalinism turns this resistance into obedience to a command structure, a form of *authority* in which various forms of populism and state-sponsored rearticulation of power relations are seen as the most effective means of change.

Eighth, Marxism values *collectivity*, collective activity as the basis for participation which is not reduced to simple equality or equivalence of each individual's voice but of subjects constituted in such a way as to be able to understand and change the world, through praxis. The bureaucracy replaces this with a cult of the personality in which great leadership individualizes resistance and subordinates it to party and state *discipline*. Ninth, Marxism is an open, self-transformative process of inquiry and change. The *reflexivity* necessary to Marxist analysis as a form of intervention is evident in its progressive recursive engagement with other social forces such as feminism and, more recently, ecological movements. Stalinism, in contrast, operates on the assumption that some version of *science* will save the day, in its most grotesque forms as an identitarian 'proletarian science'. Here, 'scientific' dialectical materialism is the path to accumulating unquestioned truth about society and nature. Finally, Marxism is a theoretical and practical articulation of the working class as it grasps the nature of alienation under capitalism and constructs its own zones of *freedom*. It aims to overcome alienated conditions of production through a revolutionary process in which there are qualitatively greater degrees of free association, in which the free association of each is dependent on the free association of all. Stalinism offers only the barest comfort in the humiliating *deference* to elders and betters; the mystifying non-dialectical opposition to capitalism as a competitor posed through the cynical and ironic complaint of those who must be positioned as victims of the bureaucracy. This is complaint sometimes expressed as the view that, however bad the exploitation of man by man is under capitalism, under the domain of the bureaucracy it is at least the other way around.

NSK

Now we turn to a cultural-political movement that developed under Stalinism in its dying days, in Slovenia in the 1980s (Monroe, 2005). This is a living laboratory, a case example through which it is possible to work through some of the contradictory and complicit relationships between Marxism and psychoanalysis.

The initials NSK stand for *Neue Slowenische Kunst* (New Slovenian Art) as a self-designation for a movement that is already marked in the German language, and so also deliberately and explicitly outside and against the domain of the bureaucracy which was founded on the resistance of the Slovene partisans against fascism. The component parts of NSK were heavily influenced by certain psychoanalytic ideas. Wilhelm Reich had already been popular as a counter-cultural force in Yugoslavia, with the film *Mysteries of the Organism* (1971) being one symptomatic connection between the East European and West European Left. There had also been widespread academic debate drawing on the tradition of the Frankfurt School, and at the end of the 1970s and beginning of the 1980s the work of Althusser and then Lacan become popular as a theoretical resource to understand and challenge the hold of the bureaucracy.

Thus NSK drew on elements of psychoanalytic theory to turn Stalinized Marxism against itself, and psychoanalysis – we could even say 'Stalinized psychoanalysis' – against itself. These are the conditions of possibility for the work of Slavoj Žižek, and it is even possible to see Žižek's political-psychoanalytic project already elaborated and played out in NSK, though it is not the task of this chapter to do that (Parker, 2007c). This cultural-political practice utilizes psychoanalysis in such a way as to disturb the relationship between psychoanalysis and the capitalist system that gave birth to it and to which it so faithfully corresponds. As we will see, the key problematic around which NSK came to operate in and against versions of Marxism and psychoanalysis was the state. Here it is the state as crystallization and sedimentation of Marxism betrayed and a micro-state in each individual citizen for whom the worst, most reactionary aspects of psychoanalysis would imprison them in it.

The first thing to note about the conditions in which the NSK developed was that the opposition movement inside Slovenia in the late 1970s actually started with mass youth rebellion. This movement unleashed creative energies against the regime, but it was clear that the resistance needed to be organized, so the question is what forms of *organization* would be necessary to combat a regime that was itself highly structured? The opposition movement started with punk, and while punk did open up possibilities for chaotic refusal of organization and any kind of centralization, the NSK project took a quite different path. The intervention of the NSK group began with the appearance of the band Laibach in the industrial town of Trbovlje in the 1980. The name was already a provocation, for 'Laibach' is the German name for the capital of Slovenia, Ljubljana. One can see a question here, but it is a question that is posed to the audience as to whether this means that Laibach are fascist. As Žižek has pointed out in some of his writings defending Laibach and NSK, like a good psychoanalyst they do not answer this question of transference (Žižek, 1993b). The organizational form thus serves to produce an enigma; it plays with existing relations of power while opening a space to question them. It renders relations of power explicit so that the audience must work through those transferential relations – the repetition of past relationships in relation to the band – themselves. For Laibach to tell the audience that this is simply a game, a ploy to expose the regime, would actually be to have fallen into the trap of endorsing that power relationship rather than unravelling it. So, closed *organization*, the cryptic organizational form produces a form of transference which turns the regime against itself. And so it keeps open the question of transference, rather than stabilizing it as a warrant for patterns of exploitation or centralization of power.

Let us turn to one of the most powerful ideological resources the Stalinist regimes used to legitimate their existence, the safeguarding of the nation and *nationality*. This is tackled by NSK in a number of ways. There is explicit participation in some of the most ridiculous romantic images of the nation. Alongside the band Laibach, a key component of NSK is the artistic group Irwin (originally known as 'R Irwin S' in a found name object taken from a Cincinnati clockmaker). Here, *nationality* as a form of identity is repeated to the point where it becomes ridiculous, and one might draw a parallel with the way the analysand speaks interminably of their 'identity', and in the process finds some distance from it. Irwin have recently initiated the NSK Garda project, and we see here a 'transnational' dimension to this Slovene cultural-political intervention that now, as Yugoslavia has been fragmented into separate nation states, questions the identity of each nation. Members of the Croatian armed forces, now separated from the other republics of Yugoslavia, pose dressed in NSK uniforms and saluting the NSK flag. This unravelling of identity is undertaken also in Kosovo with the Serb forces based there. It is further extended to the armies of the 'salarymen' in Japan, and serves to draw attention to the identity of the workforce under capitalism (and the NSK interview project with Nigerian applicants, reported in the March 2008 issue of *Reartikulacija: Umetniško-Politična-Teoretična-Diskurzivna Platforma*). Other elements of NSK also draw on nationalist imagery, to question grandiose projects of state-building and the quest for territory, for example in celebration of the entirely fictional 'Slovene Space Agency'. *Nationality* is therefore quite explicitly turned into something that needs to be constructed, and the elements from which it is constructed are quite deliberately chosen from outside the nation. The nation as a separate, discrete, essentialized identity is questioned in the very process of its production.

Submission to the nation is also disturbed even at the moment it is performed. Posters were produced and circulated by the 'Novi Kolektivizem' (NK) group of NSK in 1990 as Yugoslavia was disintegrating, and as Slovenia was being levered out from the 'socialist federation' under pressure from Germany. This was at a time when Slovenia shifted from the 'east' of Europe into the 'west', from the 'socialist stage-managed' sector into the capitalist free market, so questions of freedom and the fight for freedom in Europe were on the agenda. The solution the free market invited as it grabbed the spoils of war in Yugoslavia was, as the slogan on a Novi Kolektivizem poster put it, to 'Buy victory'. Another poster proclaimed 'I want to fight for a new Europe', but this time the poster pasted up in the streets of Ljubljana was in Croatian. The meaning of national identification is thus reduced, through repetition, to nonsense.

The posters were an intervention at a time of war that called for identification with the state and with capitalism, in such a way as to subvert both. *Submission* provides a way of embracing ideology, for it is only by offering oneself up to forms of interpellation – to the way in which one is hailed by ideology – that it is possible to take a distance from that interpellation. It is the fantasy that we have a place outside the ideology that is the most powerful lure of ideology itself, and NSK tackles this fantasy head on (Žižek, 1994).

Slovenia broke away from Yugoslavia in 1991 to become a separate *state*. This posed a question to the opposition. What forms of participation could there be in such a state that proclaimed itself to be 'independent'. The response was 'NSK State in Time', formed in 1991. This 'State in Time' has embassies around the world. It has set up consulates, in Florence in a hotel bedroom, for example. An NSK Embassy was established in Sarajevo in the mid-1990s. This embassy operated during the Laibach 'NATO Occupied Europe' tour. The NSK State in Time diplomatic passports issued in Sarajevo were realistic enough to enable people to escape Bosnia–Herzegovina during the civil war. Submission to symbolic forms that define identity is thus reworked. Here NSK mobilized elements of dominant symbolic structures that send a message to the individual subject that 'you are this', but they turn this message back into a reply that 'we are this'. And this message in reverse simultaneously twists the clinical structure of those addressed beyond contained guilty obsessional adherence to open hysterical defiance. In psychoanalytic terms, this is defiance that includes the subject within it, for now this is as deliberate participation rather than by adopting the position of victim (Žižek, 1993a).

The NSK State in Time issues its own stamps. In addition to the nskstate.com website, there are passport offices that issue passports. To obtain a passport in one of the passport offices is a long and laborious process. The process reproduces the apparatus of the state and submission to the state inside the art installation. Citizens of NSK, who number more than those of the Vatican City, are not members of NSK, and not all citizens have diplomatic passports. The 'integrity' of the state is questioned from within, within the very procedures of enunciation which declare it to be a state. The first inside page of the passport has the phrase 'art is fanaticism that demands diplomacy'. Here a psychoanalytic model of the subject, fanatically adhering to the identifications that comprise it, is turned against itself in the call for a 'diplomatic relation' with others. This, remember, is against the context in which 'diplomacy' between the Stalinist bureaucracy in the Soviet Union and friendly capitalist nations functioned to seal over the conflicts on both sides of the border that divided them. Calls for unity inside the Soviet Union went hand in hand with alliances with the state apparatus on the part of communist parties working to support diplomatic deals between friendly nations and the Soviet Union. This alternative *state* is not democratic, and does not pretend to be so.

The NSK State is a symbolic apparatus. It has been claimed by Žižek that, as Yugoslavia disintegrated, the NSK State provided a symbolic state form which did not correspond to geographical territory. Some of the key symbolic resources are drawn from Russian *Suprematism* (Arns, 2003). Founded by Kazimir Malevich in 1915, Suprematism is useful for a number of reasons. First, there is a reduction to pure form, meaningless figures that are then injected with content, and so Suprematism provides visual correlates of a Saussurean approach to language in which the visual signifiers are reduced to nonsense, absolute difference that analysts might aim for at the end of analysis. Second, Malevich was incorporated by the Bolsheviks into avant-garde art after the revolution, even though he was not revolutionary. There is therefore a political ambiguity built into Suprematism as an art movement. Third, Malevich is a Russian artist, and so the symbolic material of a Slovenian art movement, NSK, is built out of external resources, and, a further twist, Malevich was not actually Russian but Ukrainian.

Suprematism produces its own meaningless representative symbols, such as the Black Square. Malevich's Black Cross also has a useful ambiguous connotative relation to anarchism and Christianity. These Suprematist elements are incorporated into NSK art, including in the Irwin installations. The Black Cross is then exported to different contexts, for example on the skyscrapers of New York. The NSK response to the 9/11 attacks was the US tour called 'Divided States of America' with the slogan 'United we fall'. Suprematism revels in the way we are determined as subjects by material that we may understand to be 'unconscious', material that we cannot escape but which we can forge a different relationship with. Suprematism thus provides a matrix within which other ideological elements can be articulated.

The NSK State is a State in Time, not in geographical territory, and so *temporality* is one of the governing devices of NSK. The 2003 Laibach album was called *WAT*, which stands for 'We Are Time'. Symbolic resources for this state are taken from the past as well as from outside Slovenia. The Black Cross is resignified in the context of Kitsch images of Landseer deer, for example. There is also use of National Socialist art mixed together with Socialist Realist iconography. The Black Square is repeated in different contexts to disturb and create moments of ambiguity (Gržnic, 2004). The 'time' element is worked in different ways in different elements of NSK, but always with an element of 'retroactivity'. Here there is reworking of psychoanalytic conceptions of time, of *temporality* as a cultural-political analytic form, against linear conceptions.

One of the key political strategies of NSK is a particular take on identification with power which is often termed 'overidentification'. This utilizes and subverts *adaptation.* Overidentification is not simple parody, but brings the opposition much closer to the imagery that is being reproduced and reworked. Western cultural material, which seems innocent, is incorporated and reworked. This material is twisted, so for example, 'Get back, get back to where you once belonged', sung in heavy metal tones on Laibach's cover of the Beatles' *Let it Be* album draws out latently authoritarian and xenophobic significations, and the phrase 'nothing's going to change my world' (from the track 'Across the Universe') is resignified in line with fascist imagery of the nation.

The title of the Laibach album *Volk* evokes, of course, community and nationalist conceptions of the people. '*Volk*' in Slovene also means 'wolf'. The album comprises twists on national anthems, some with changes of wording, some with very few changes but in a way that draws attention to latent imagery within the anthems. The English anthem, 'Anglia', for example, is a taunting 'God save your gracious queen' which follows the description of imperialism and torture conducted by the British state. The most well-known example of overidentification was through the Novi

Kolektivizem contribution for 1987 National Youth day, which was praised by the panel of judges for evoking the spirit of Yugoslav socialist youth. The 'poster scandal' erupted when it was revealed that the NK poster was based on a 1936 Nazi poster. The message about the regime was thus returned to it in reverse: 'you say you are this, you are this.'

Overidentification thus reproduces, in a voluntary submission to ideology, what the regime requires. The regime requires that there is also some cynical distance. Ideology works not only by people adhering to it, but by their believing that they have some freedom to do so, and so the phenomenon of 'dissidence' in Eastern Europe provided a buffer zone between citizens and the state. Overidentification dissolves this buffer zone and disturbs an attempt at *adaptation*. It could be said that it brings subjects closer to an 'identification with the symptom' which, by virtue of that identification, embraces and dissolves its grip (Žižek, 2005). Voluntary submission to authority in the NSK State which is not a democratic state requires that bourgeois individuality is opposed. NSK projects are *group* projects. In the early years all statements were group statements, and members of the band Laibach had changing personnel. Laibach thus presented an enigma about identity. The '*group*' revealed the truth of the particular identifications that a subject adopts in order to produce themselves as if they were separate, distinct.

There is thus also an aspect of deliberate *mystification* in NSK activities, and certainly no claim to transparency or 'understanding'. The NSK State in Time comprises 'state artists', which is the Irwin group, 'state politicians', which is the band Laibach, and a 'state church', which is the theatre group Cosmokinetic Theatre Noordung. Theatre performances include confining the audience so their heads are between planks of the stage, and sacramental wine and wafers are forced into their mouths by the performers. It should be remembered that, unlike most of Yugoslavia, Slovenia is a Catholic country, so religious imagery, and the Black Cross for example, are quite deliberate provocations. The *mystification* is the setting for more intense identification. The identification provoked by NSK State practices mobilizes *enjoyment*: NSK uses its imagery in order to produce enjoyable identification, and overidentification with what is worst in ideology. This is what provokes accusations that Laibach is fascist, a fascism beautifully enacted, for example' in 'Tanz Mit Laibach' on the *WAT* album. Thus NSK uses and plays with fascist imagery. Such *enjoyment* takes it to the limits of psychoanalysis, and beyond.

Conclusions

The precise interrelationship between psychoanalysis and NSK strategy is ambiguous, so that not even psychoanalysis operates as a worldview that can pretend to escape from ideology. The NSK State provokes uncertainty and refuses the coordinates of capitalism and classical Marxism, and, of course, Stalinism, even though it must necessarily repeat some of those motifs. The characterization I have given of capitalism can be contested of course, and the way we define the enemy also serves to define how we will seek to overcome it. The shape of the grid, and the way capitalism is given shape from the standpoint of Marxism, means that the cultural-political project of NSK is also given a certain definition, a shape that will also constrain it. Just as it questions the state from within its own given parameters, however, NSK was formed to contest hegemonic conceptualizations of the state in relation to capitalism – the formation of the Yugoslav state out of victorious partisan struggle that also overthrew capitalism – and then in relation to psychoanalysis, formed under capitalism as both an interrogation of and confirmation of bourgeois subjectivity and then imported into the cultural matrix of Stalinism.

The NSK operates as a form of mediation between psychoanalysis and Marxism that treats the relationship between the two traditions of practical critique as a dialectical relationship. A dialectical relationship needs to be handled conceptually and politically in dialectical terms, and as part of a historical-materialist analysis of and intervention into capitalism and the bureaucratic pretenders to an alternative to capitalism. That is, the relationship cannot be mediated in such a way as to merely plug the gaps between two different views of the world, to seal over the divisions between the two or to enable each practice to complement each other. Instead, NSK mediates by functioning as an *obstacle* to any harmonious relationship between Marxists and psychoanalysts. In this way, in these particular conditions, it re-energizes aspects of psychoanalysis and even of Marxism, and it does this by reorganizing cultural-political action in relation to the state. It is not Marxist, but it opens a space once again for Marxism in conditions scarred by Stalinism. It is not psychoanalytic, but it opens a space for forms of psychoanalytic practice that do not invite a return to capitalism as a way out from Stalinism.

References

Adlam, D., Henriques, J., Rose, N., Salfield, A., Venn, C., and Walkerdine, V. (1977) 'Psychology, ideology and the human subject', *Ideology and Consciousness*, 1, 5–56.

Althusser, L. (1971) *Lenin and Philosophy, and Other Essays*. London: New Left Books.

Arns, I. (ed.) (2003) *Irwin: Retroprincip*. Frankfurt: Revolver.

Ashcroft, B., Griffiths, G. and Tiffin, H. (eds) (1995) *The Post-Colonial Studies Reader*. London: Routledge.

Bensaïd, D. (2002) *Marx for Our Times: Adventures and Misadventures of a Critique*. London: Verso.

Bertoldi, A. (1998) 'Oedipus in (South) Africa?: Psychoanalysis and the politics of difference', *American Imago*, 55, 101–134.

Bettelheim, B. (1986) *Freud and Man's Soul*. London: Flamingo.

Billig, M. (1976) *Social Psychology and Intergroup Relations*. London: Academic Press.

Billig, M. (1999) *Freudian Repression: Conversation Creating the Unconscious*. Cambridge: Cambridge University Press.

Blackman, L. (1994) 'What is doing history? The use of history to understand the constitution of contemporary psychological objects', in I. Parker (ed.) (2011) *Critical Psychology: Critical Concepts in Psychology, Vol. 4, Alternatives and Visions for Change*. Abingdon and New York: Routledge.

Bourne, B., Eichler, U. and Herman, D. (eds) (1987) *Voices: Psychoanalysis*. Nottingham: Spokesman/Hobo Press.

Branney, P. (2008) 'Subjectivity, not personality: Combining discourse analysis and psychoanalysis', in I. Parker (ed.) (2011) *Critical Psychology: Critical Concepts in Psychology, Volume 4, Alternatives and Visions for Change* (pp. 262–269). London and New York: Routledge.

Breuer, J. and Freud, S. (1895) 'Studies on hysteria', in S. Freud (1966–1974) *The Standard Edition of the Complete Psychological Works of Sigmund Freud, Vol. II* (translated by J. Strachey). London: Vintage, The Hogarth Press and the Institute of Psycho-Analysis.

Britzman, D. (2011) *Freud and Education*. London: Routledge.

Brousse, M.-H. (2004) 'Psychoanalysis and the therapy market', *Mental Online: International Journal of Mental Health and Applied Psychoanalysis*, 14.

Brown, S.D., Pujol, J. and Curt, B.C. (1998) 'As one in a web? Discourse, materiality and the place of ethics', in I. Parker (ed.) *Social Constructionism, Discourse and Realism.* London: Sage.

Burgoyne, B. (1997) 'Interpretation', in B. Burgoyne and M. Sullivan (eds) *The Klein–Lacan Dialogues*. London: Rebus Press.

Burgoyne, B. and Sullivan, M. (eds) (1997) *The Klein–Lacan Dialogues.* London: Rebus Press.

Burman, E. (1997) 'Review of *Closely Observed Infants*', *Changes*, 15(4), 292–293.

Burman, E. (1998) 'Children, false memories, and disciplinary alliances: Tensions between developmental psychology and psychoanalysis', *Psychoanalysis and Contemporary Thought*, 31, 307–333.

Burman, E. (2008) *Deconstructing Developmental Psychology*, 2nd edn. Abingdon and New York: Routledge.

Burman, E., and Frosh, S. (eds) (2005) 'Contemporary debates in social theory' (special issue), *Group Analysis*, 38(1).

Clarke, S. and Hoggett, P. (eds) (2009) *Researching Beneath the Surface: Psycho-Social Research Methods in Practice*. London: Karnac.

Coltart, N. (2000) *Slouching towards Bethlehem.* New York: The Other Press.

Coppola, S. (dir. 2003) *Lost in Translation* (film).

Cottet, S. (1993) 'Should we analyse the transference?', *Journal of the Centre for Freudian Analysis and Research*, 2, 3–10.

Couve, C. (1986) 'Psychology and politics in Manganyi's work: A materialist critique', *Psychology in Society*, 5, 90–130.

Crossley, M. (2004) 'Making sense of "barebacking": Gay men's narratives, unsafe sex and the "resistance habitus"', *British Journal of Social Psychology*, 43, 225–244.

Cushman, P. (1991) 'Ideology obscured: Political uses of the self in Daniel Stern's infant', in I. Parker (ed.) (2011) *Critical Psychology: Critical Concepts in Psychology, Vol. 3, Psychologisation and Psychological Culture*. Abingdon and New York: Routledge.

Dafermos, M., Marvakis, A. and Triliva, S. (eds.) (2006) 'Critical psychology in a changing world: Contributions from different geo-political regions', special issue, *Annual Review of Critical Psychology*, 5.

Dafermos, M., Marvakis, A., Mentinis, M., Painter, D. and Triliva, S. (eds) (2013) 'Critical psychology in a changing world: Building bridges and expanding the dialogue', special issue, *Annual Review of Critical Psychology*, 10.

Dalal, F. (1988) 'The racism of Jung', in I. Parker (ed.) (2011) *Critical Psychology: Critical Concepts in Psychology, Vol. 1, Dominant Models of Psychology and Their Limits*. Abingdon and New York: Routledge.

Danziger, K. (1997) *Naming the Mind: How Psychology Found Its Language.* London: Sage.

Davids, M.F. (1996) 'Frantz Fanon: the struggle for inner freedom', *Free Associations*, 6(2)(38), 205–234.

De Vos, J. (2008) 'From Panopticon to pan-psychologisation or, Why do so many women study psychology?', *International Journal of Žižek Studies*, 2(1), 1–18.

De Vos, J. (2012) *Psychologisation in Times of Globalisation*. Abingdon and New York: Routledge.

Derrida, J. (1988) 'Geopsychoanalysis: ". . . and the rest of the world"', in C. Lane (ed.) *The Psychoanalysis of Race*. New York: Columbia University Press.

Dunker, C. (2005) 'Truth structured like fiction: Sexual theories of children viewed as narrative', *Journal for Lacanian Studies*, 2, 183–197.

Dunker, C. and Parker, I. (2009) 'How to be secretly Lacanian in anti-psychoanalytic qualitative research', *Annual Review of Critical Psychology*, 7, 52–71.

Fairfield, S., Layton, L. and Stack, C. (eds) (2002) *Bringing the Plague: Toward a Postmodern Psychoanalysis*. New York: Other Press.

Fanon, F. (1967) *The Wretched of the Earth*. Harmondsworth: Penguin.

Fanon, F. (1986) *Black Skins, White Masks*. London: Pluto Press.

Fink, B. (1997) *A Clinical Introduction to Lacanian Psychoanalysis: Theory and Technique*. Cambridge, MA: Harvard University Press.

Fink, B. (2007) *Fundamentals of Psychoanalytic Technique: A Lacanian Approach for Practitioners*. New York: W.W. Norton.

Fink, B. (2004a) 'Lacan in "translation"', *Journal for Lacanian Studies*, 2(2), 254–281.

Fink, B. (2004b) *Lacan to the Letter: Reading* Écrits *Closely*. Minneapolis: University of Minnesota Press.

Finlay, L. and Gough, B. (eds) (2003) *Reflexivity: A Practical Guide for Researchers in Health and Social Sciences*. Oxford: Blackwell.

Fonagy, P. (2000) 'The outcome of psychoanalysis: The hope of a future', *The Psychologist*, 13, 620–623.

Fonagy, P. and Target, M. (2004) 'What can developmental psychopathology tell psychoanalysts about the mind?', in A. Casement (ed.) *Who Owns Psychoanalysis?* London: Karnac.

Fonagy, P., Gergely, G., Jurist, E.L. and Target, M. (2004) *Affect Regulation, Mentalization, and the Development of Self*. London: Karnac.

Forrester, J. (1997) *Dispatches from the Freud Wars: Psychoanalysis and Its Passions*. Boston, MA: Harvard University Press.

Foucault, M. (1969/1972) *The Archaeology of Knowledge*. London: Tavistock Publications.

Freud, A. (1936) *The Ego and the Mechanisms of Defence*. London: The Hogarth Press.

Freud, S. (1900/1999) *The Interpretation of Dreams* (translated by J. Crick). Oxford: Oxford University Press.

Freud, S. (1907) 'Obsessive actions and religious practices', in S. Freud (1966–1974) *The Standard Edition of the Complete Psychological Works of Sigmund Freud, Vol. IX* (translated by J. Strachey). London: Vintage, The Hogarth Press and the Institute of Psycho-Analysis.

Freud, S. (1915) 'Observations on transference-love (further recommendations on the technique of psycho-analysis III)', in S. Freud (1966–1974) *The Standard Edition of the Complete Psychological Works of Sigmund Freud, Vol. XII* (translated by J. Strachey). London: Vintage, The Hogarth Press and the Institute of Psycho-Analysis.

Freud, S. (1918 [1914]) 'From the history of an infantile neurosis', in S. Freud (1966–1974) *The Standard Edition of the Complete Psychological Works of Sigmund Freud, Vol. XVII* (translated by J. Strachey). London: Vintage, The Hogarth Press and the Institute of Psycho-Analysis.

Freud, S. (1921) 'Group psychology and the analysis of the ego', in S. Freud (1966–1974) *The Standard Edition of the Complete Psychological Works of Sigmund Freud, Vol. XVIII* (translated by J. Strachey). London: Vintage, The Hogarth Press and the Institute of Psycho-Analysis.

Freud, S. (1925) 'Negation', in S. Freud (1966–1974) *The Standard Edition of the Complete Psychological Works of Sigmund Freud, Vol. XIX* (translated by J. Strachey). London: Vintage, The Hogarth Press and the Institute of Psycho-Analysis.

Freud, S. (1926) 'The Question of lay analysis', in S. Freud (1966–1974) *The Standard Edition of the Complete Psychological Works of Sigmund Freud, Vol. XX* (translated by J. Strachey). London: Vintage, The Hogarth Press and the Institute of Psycho-Analysis.

Freud, S. (1930 [1929]) 'Civilization and its discontents', in S. Freud (1966–1974) *The Standard Edition of the Complete Psychological Works of Sigmund Freud, Vol. XXI* (translated by J. Strachey). London: Vintage, The Hogarth Press and the Institute of Psycho-Analysis.

Freud, S. (1933) 'New introductory lectures on psycho-analysis', in S. Freud (1966–1974) *The Standard Edition of the Complete Psychological Works of Sigmund Freud, Vol. XXII* (translated by J. Strachey). London: Vintage, The Hogarth Press and the Institute of Psycho-Analysis.

Freud, S. (1937) 'Analysis terminable and interminable', in S. Freud (1966–1974) *The Standard Edition of the Complete Psychological Works of Sigmund Freud, Vol. XXIII* (translated by J. Strachey). London: Vintage, The Hogarth Press and the Institute of Psycho-Analysis.

Freud, S. (1953–1974) *The Standard Edition of the Complete Psychological Works of Sigmund Freud* (24 vols) (translated by J. Strachey). London: Vintage, The Hogarth Press and the Institute of Psycho-Analysis.

Froggett, L. and Wengraf, T. (2004) 'Interpreting interviews in the light of research team dynamics: A study of Nila's biographic narrative', *International Journal of Critical Psychology*, 10, 94–122.

Frosh, S. (1989) *Psychoanalysis and Psychology: Minding the Gap.* London: Macmillan.

Frosh, S. (2002) *After Words: The Personal in Gender, Culture and Psychotherapy.* London: Palgrave.

Frosh, S. (2005) *Hate and the 'Jewish science': Anti-Semitism, Nazism, and Psychoanalysis.* London: Palgrave.

Frosh, S. and Baraitser, L. (2008) 'Psychoanalysis and psychosocial studies', *Psychoanalysis, Culture and Society*, 13, 346–365.

Frosh, S., Phoenix, A. and Pattman, R. (2001) *Young Masculinities*. Basingstoke and New York: Palgrave.

Frosh, S., Phoenix, A. and Pattman, R. (2003) 'Taking a stand: Using psychoanalysis to explore the positioning of subjects in discourse', *British Journal of Social Psychology*, 42, 39–53.

Gallagher, C. (2005) 'Re-Englishing *Encore*', *The Letter: Lacanian Perspectives on Psychoanalysis*, 33, 1–21.

Gardiner, M. (ed.) (1972) *The Wolf-Man and Sigmund Freud.* London: Hogarth Press.

Gay, P. (1988) *Freud: A Life for Our Time.* New York: W.W. Norton.

Gergen, K. J. (1985) 'The social constructionist movement in modern psychology', *American Psychologist*, 40, 266–275.

Gergen, K.J. (1991) *The Saturated Self: Dilemmas of Identity in Contemporary Life.* New York: Basic Books.

Glynos, J. and Y. Stavrakakis (2002) 'Postures and impostures: On Lacan's style and use of mathematical structure', in J. Glynos and A. Stravrakakis (eds) *Lacan and Science*. London: Karnac.

Gržnic, M. (2004) *Situated Contemporary Art Practices: Art, Theory and Activism from (the East of) Europe*. Ljubljana: Založba ZRC.

Gueguen, P.-G. (1995) 'Transference as deception', in R. Feldstein, B. Fink and M. Jaanus (eds) *Reading Seminar XI: Lacan's Four Fundamental Concepts of Psychoanalysis*. New York: SUNY Press.

Gülerce, A. (2005) 'Anxiety and phantasy as psychopolitical agents of resistance: Converging Klein and Lacan on theorizing subjectivity and society', in A. Gülerce, A. Hofmeister, I. Steauble, G. Saunders and J. Kaye (eds) *Contemporary Theorizing in Psychology: Global Perspectives.* Concord, ON: Captus Press Inc.

Haaken, J. (1998) *Pillar of Salt: Gender, Memory, and the Perils of Looking Back.* New Brunswick, NJ: Rutgers University Press.

Haraway, D. (1989) 'Metaphors into hardware: Harry Harlow and the technology of love', in I. Parker (ed.) (2011) *Critical Psychology: Critical Concepts in Psychology, Vol. 1, Dominant Models of Psychology and Their Limits*. Abingdon and New York: Routledge.

Harré, R. (2004) 'Staking our claim for qualitative psychology as science', in I. Parker (ed.) (2011) *Critical Psychology: Critical Concepts in Psychology, Vol. 2, Contradictions in Psychology and Elements of Resistance*. Abingdon and New York: Routledge.

Harré, R. and Secord, P.F. (1972) *The Explanation of Social Behaviour*. Oxford: Basil Blackwell.

Hartmann, H. (1939/1958) *Ego Psychology and the Problem of Adaptation.* New York: International Universities Press.

Hayes, G. (1989) 'Psychology and ideology: The case of Althusser', *South African Journal of Psychology*, 19(2), 84–90.

Hayes, G. (1998) 'We suffer our memories: Thinking about the past, healing and reconciliation', in I. Parker (ed.) (2011) *Critical Psychology: Critical Concepts in Psychology, Vol. 2, Contradictions in Psychology and Elements of Resistance*. Abingdon and New York: Routledge.

Hayes, G. (2002) 'Sachs, Chavafambira, Maggie: Prurience or the pathology of social relations?', *South African Journal of Psychology*, 32(2), 43–48.

Heelas, P. and Lock, A. (eds) (1981) *Indigenous Psychologies: The Anthropology of the Self.* London: Academic Press.

Heimann, P. (1950) 'On countertransference', *International Journal of Psycho-Analysis*, 31, 81–84.

Henriques, J., Hollway, W., Urwin, C., Venn, C. and Walkerdine, V. (1984/1998) *Changing the Subject: Psychology, Social Regulation and Subjectivity.* London and New York: Routledge.

Hinshelwood, R. (1997) 'Transference and counter-transference', in B. Burgoyne and M. Sullivan (eds) *The Klein–Lacan Dialogues.* London: Rebus Press.

Hollway, W. (1989) *Subjectivity and Method in Psychology: Gender, Meaning and Science.* London: Sage.

Hollway, W. (2008) 'The importance of relational thinking in the practice of psycho-social research: Ontology, epistemology, methodology and ethics', in S. Clarke, P. Hoggett and H. Hahn (eds) *Object Relations and Social Relations.* London: Karnac.

Hollway, W. and Jefferson, T. (2000) *Doing Qualitative Research Differently: Free Association, Narrative and the Interview Method.* London: Sage.

Hollway, W. and Jefferson, T. (2005) 'Panic and perjury: A psychosocial exploration of agency', *British Journal of Social Psychology*, 44, 147–163.

Hook, D. (2005) 'Genealogy, discourse, "effective history": Foucault and the work of critique', *Qualitative Research in Psychology*, 2, 3–31.

Hook, D. (2006) '"Pre-discursive" racism', *Journal of Community and Applied Social Psychology*, 16, 207–232.

Hook, D. (2011) *A Critical Psychology of the Postcolonial: The Mind of Apartheid.* London: Routledge.

Hunt, J.C. (1989) *Psychoanalytic Aspects of Fieldwork* (Sage University Paper Series on Qualitative Methods, Vol. 18). Beverley Hills, CA: Sage.

Hyppolite, J. (1956) 'A spoken commentary on Freud's "Verneinung"', in J. Lacan (2006) *Écrits: The First Complete Edition in English* (translated with notes by B. Fink in collaboration with H. Fink and R. Grigg). New York: W.W. Norton.

Immelman, A. (1999) 'Inside the mind of Milosevic', Unit for the Study of Personality in Politics, St John's University, Collegeville, MN, http://www1.csbsju.edu/uspp/Milosevic/Milosevic.html (accessed 7 March 2014).

Immelman, A. (2003) 'Psychological profile of Saddam Hussein', Unit for the Study of Personality in Politics, St John's University, Collegeville, MN, http://www1.csbsju.edu/uspp/Research/Saddam%20profile.html (accessed 7 March 2014)

Ingleby, D. (1985) 'Professionals as socializers: The "psy complex"', in I. Parker (ed.) (2011) *Critical Psychology: Critical Concepts in Psychology, Vol. 1, Dominant Models of Psychology and Their Limits.* Abingdon and New York: Routledge.

International Psychoanalytic Association (2006) 'Constituent and other organizations', http://www.ipa.org.uk/site/cms/contentViewArticle.asp?article=1054 (accessed 16 June 2006).

Jacoby, R. (1975) *Social Amnesia: A Critique of Conformist Psychology from Adler to Laing.* New York: Beacon Press.

Jacoby, R. (1983) *The Repression of Psychoanalysis.* New York: Basic Books.

Jones, R.A. (2003) 'Mixed metaphors and narrative shifts: Archetypes', *Theory & Psychology*, 13, 651–672.

Jung, C.G. (1983) *Jung: Selected Writings*. London: Fontana.

Jung, C.G. (1989) *Aspects of the Masculine*. London: Routledge.

Kaës, R. (1984) 'Representation and mentalization: From the represented group to the group process', in R.M. Farr and S. Moscovici (eds) *Social Representations*. Cambridge: Cambridge University Press.

Kareem, J. and Littlewood, R. (1999) *Intercultural Therapy: Themes, Interpretations and Practice*. Oxford: Blackwell.

Klein, M. (1986) *The Selected Melanie Klein* (edited by J. Mitchell). Harmondsworth: Peregrine.

Klotz, J.-P. (1995) 'The passionate dimension of transference', in R. Feldstein, B. Fink, and M. Jaanus (eds) *Reading Seminar XI: Lacan's Four Fundamental Concepts of Psychoanalysis*. New York: SUNY Press.

Kottler, A. (1997) 'Homosexuality and psychoanalytic training: Struggles in England and North America – what implications for South Africa?', *Psychology in Society*, 22, 5–26.

Kovel, J. (1974) 'Erik Erikson's psychohistory', in I. Parker (ed.) (2011) *Critical Psychology: Critical Concepts in Psychology, Vol. 1, Dominant Models of Psychology and Their Limits*. Abingdon and New York: Routledge.

Kovel, J. (1988) *The Radical Spirit: Essays on Psychoanalysis and Society*. London: Free Association Books.

Kris, E. (1951) 'Ego psychology and interpretation in psychoanalytic therapy', *Psychoanalytic Quarterly*, 21(1), 15–30.

Kvale, S. (1996) *InterViews: An Introduction to Qualitative Research Interviewing*. London: Sage.

Lacan, J. (1952) 'Intervention on transference', in J. Mitchell and J. Rose (eds) (1982) *Feminine Sexuality: Jacques Lacan and the école freudienne*. London: Macmillan.

Lacan, J. (1953) 'The function and field of speech and language in psychoanalysis', in J. Lacan (2006) *Écrits: The First Complete Edition in English* (translated with notes by Bruce Fink in collaboration with Héloïse Fink and Russell Grigg) New York: W.W. Norton.

Lacan, J. (1956) 'Response to Jean Hyppolite's commentary on Freud's "*Verneinung*"', in J. Lacan (2006) *Écrits: The First Complete Edition in English* (translated with notes by Bruce Fink in collaboration with Héloïse Fink and Russell Grigg) New York: W.W. Norton.

Lacan, J. (1958) 'The direction of the treatment and the principles of its power', in J. Lacan (2006) *Écrits: The First Complete Edition in English* (translated with notes by Bruce Fink in collaboration with Héloïse Fink and Russell Grigg) New York: W.W. Norton.

Lacan, J. (1960–1961) *The Seminar of Jacques Lacan Book VIII, Transference*, translated by Cormac Gallagher from unedited French manuscripts. Unpublished. (Versions of the Gallagher translation are updated from time to time and available at http://www.lacaninireland.com.)

Lacan, J. (1961–1962) *The Seminar of Jacques Lacan Book IX, Identification*. Translated by Cormac Gallagher from unedited French manuscripts. Unpublished.

(Versions of the Gallagher translation are updated from time to time and available at http://www.lacaninireland.com.)

Lacan, J. (1964/1973) *The Four Fundamental Concepts of Psycho-Analysis: The Seminar of Jacques Lacan, Book XI* (translated by A. Sheridan). Harmondsworth: Penguin.

Lacan, J. (1975/1988) *On Feminine Sexuality, The Limits of Love and Knowledge, 1972–1973: Encore, The Seminar of Jacques Lacan, Book XX* (translated by B. Fink). New York: W.W. Norton.

Lacan, J. (1975/1991) *The Seminar of Jacques Lacan: Book I, Freud's Papers on Technique 1953–1954* (translated with notes by J. Forrester). New York: W.W. Norton.

Lacan, J. (1977) *Écrits: A Selection* (translated by A. Sheridan). London: Tavistock.

Lacan, J. (1991/2007) *The Other Side of Psychoanalysis: The Seminar of Jacques Lacan, Book XVII* (translated with notes by R. Grigg) New York: W.W. Norton.

Lacan, J. (2006) *Écrits: The First Complete Edition in English* (translated by B. Fink, H. Fink and R. Grigg) New York: W.W. Norton.

Laplanche, J. (1999) *Essays on Otherness*. London: Routledge.

Laplanche, J. and Pontalis, J. B. (1988) *The Language of Psychoanalysis*. London: Karnac Books and the Institute of Psycho-Analysis.

Leader, D. (2000) *Freud's Footnotes*. London: Faber and Faber.

Lieven, E. (1981) '"If it's natural, we can't change it"', in I. Parker (ed.) (2011) *Critical Psychology: Critical Concepts in Psychology, Vol. 1, Dominant Models of Psychology and Their Limits*. Abingdon and New York: Routledge.

Malone, K.R. (2000) 'Subjectivity and the address to the other: A Lacanian view of some impasses in theory and psychology', *Theory & Psychology*, 10, 79–86.

Malone, K.R. and Friedlander, S.R. (eds) (2000) *The Subject of Lacan: A Lacanian Reader for Psychologists*. New York: SUNY Press.

Malone, K.R., and Kelly, S.D. (2004) 'The transfer from the clinical to the social and back', *Psychoanalysis, Culture and Society*, 9, 23–32.

Mama, A. (1995) *Beyond the Masks: Race, Gender and Subjectivity*. London: Routledge.

Mandel, E. (1978) *From Stalinism to Eurocommunism: The Bitter Fruits of 'Socialism in One Country'*. London: New Left Books.

Mangabeira, W.C. (1999) 'On the textuality of objects in disciplinary practice: The couch in psychoanalysis', *Psychoanalytic Studies*, 1(3), 327–354.

Manganyi, H.C. (1973) *Being-Black-in-the-World*. Johannesburg: Ravan Press.

Mannoni, O. (1990) *Prospero and Caliban: The Psychology of Colonization*. Ann Arbor: University of Michigan Press.

Martín-Baró, I. (1994) *Writings for a Liberation Psychology*. Cambridge, MA: Harvard University Press.

Mather, R. (1997) 'On the mythology of the reflexive subject', *History of the Human Sciences*, 10(4), 65–82.

Miller, J.-A. (1986) '*Extimité*', in, M. Bracher, M.W. Alcorn, R. J. Corthell and F. Massardier-Kenney (eds) (1994) *Lacanian Theory of Discourse: Subject, Structure and Society*, New York: New York University Press.

Miller, J.-A. (1998) 'Report for the General Assembly in Barcelona – 23 July 1998', *Psychoanalytical Notebooks of the London Circle*, 1, 117–152.

Miller, J.-A. (1999) 'Interpretation in reverse', *Psychoanalytical Notebooks of the London Circle*, 2, 9–18.

Miller, L., Rustin, M. and Shuttleworth, J. (eds) (1989) *Closely Observed Infants*. London: Duckworth.

Miller, M. (1998) *Freud and the Bolsheviks: Psychoanalysis in Imperial Russia and the Soviet Union*. New Haven, CT: Yale University Press.

Miller, P. and Rose, N. (1988) 'The Tavistock programme: Governing subjectivity and social life', *Sociology*, 22, 171–192.

Miller, P. and Rose, N. (1994) 'On therapeutic authority: Psychoanalytic expertise under advanced liberalism', *History of the Human Sciences*, 7(3), 29–64.

Mitchell, J. (1974) *Psychoanalysis and Feminism*. London: Allen Lane.

Mitchell, J. (1986) 'Introduction', in J. Mitchell (ed.) *The Selected Melanie Klein*. Harmondsworth: Peregrine.

Monroe, A. (2005) *Interrogation Machine: Laibach and the NSK State*. Cambridge, MA: MIT Press.

Moscovici, S. (1976/2008) *Psychoanalysis: Its Image and Its Public* (translated by D. Macey). Cambridge: Polity Press.

Nasio, J.-D. (1998) *Five Lessons on the Psychoanalytic Theory of Jacques Lacan*. New York: SUNY Press.

Nobus, D. (2000) *Jacques Lacan and the Freudian Practice of Psychoanalysis*. London: Routledge.

Nobus, D. and Quinn, M. (2005) *Knowing Nothing, Staying Stupid: Elements for a Psychoanalytic Epistemology*. London: Routledge.

Olson, F. (2006) 'Social construction in community development in the Spring Branch, Memorial community of Houston, Texas', The Taos Institute, http://www.taosinstitute.net/Websites/taos/Images/ProgramsTaosTilburgDissertations/olson_study.pdf (accessed 7 March 2014).

Palomera, V. (1997) 'On counter-transference', in B. Burgoyne and M. Sullivan (eds) *The Klein–Lacan Dialogues*. London: Rebus Press.

Parker, I. (1989) *The Crisis in Modern Social Psychology, and How to End It*. London: Routledge.

Parker, I. (1992) *Discourse Dynamics: Critical Analysis for Social and Individual Psychology*. London: Routledge.

Parker, I. (1997) *Psychoanalytic Culture: Psychoanalytic Discourse in Western Society*. London: Sage.

Parker, I. (1999a) 'Critical Psychology: Critical links', *Annual Review of Critical Psychology*, 1, 3–18.

Parker, I. (1999b) 'Clinical Lacan: Review essay on Bruce Fink's *A Clinical Introduction to Lacanian Psychoanalysis: Theory and Technique*', *PS: Journal of the Universities Association for Psychoanalytic Studies*, 2(2), 69–74.

Parker, I. (2002) *Critical Discursive Psychology*. London: Palgrave.

Parker, I. (2003a) 'Jacques Lacan, barred psychologist', *Theory and Psychology*, 13(1), 95–115.

Parker, I. (2003b) 'Psychoanalytic narratives: Writing the self into contemporary cultural phenomena', *Narrative Inquiry*, 13(2), 301–15.

Parker, I. (2005) *Qualitative Psychology: Introducing Radical Research.* Buckingham: Open University Press.

Parker, I. (2007a) *Revolution in Psychology: Alienation to Emancipation.* London: Pluto Press.

Parker, I. (2007b) 'Lacanian psychoanalysis and revolutionary Marxism', *Lacanian Ink*, 29, 121–139.

Parker, I. (2007c) 'The truth about overidentification'', in P. Bowman and R. Stamp (eds) *The Truth of Žižek.* New York: Continuum.

Parker, I. (2008) *Japan in Analysis: Cultures of the Unconscious.* London: Palgrave.

Parker, I. (2009) *Psychoanalytic Mythologies*. London: Anthem Press.

Parker, I. (ed.) (2011a) *Critical Psychology: Critical Concepts in Psychology* (4 vols). Abingdon and New York: Routledge.

Parker, I. (2011b) *Lacanian Psychoanalysis: Revolutions in Subjectivity*. Abingdon and New York: Routledge.

Plon, M. (1974) 'On the meaning of the notion of conflict and its study in social psychology', in I. Parker (ed.) (2011) *Critical Psychology: Critical Concepts in Psychology, Vol. 2, Contradictions in Psychology and Elements of Resistance.* Abingdon and New York: Routledge.

Politzer, G. (1994) *Critique of the Foundations of Psychology: The Psychology of Psychoanalysis*. Pittsburgh, PA.: Duquesne University Press.

Power, L. and Pilgrim, D. (1990) 'The fee in psychotherapy: Practitioners' accounts', *Counselling Psychology Quarterly*, 3(2), 153–170.

Reich, W. (1946/1975) *The Mass Psychology of Fascism.* New York: Penguin.

Reich, W. (1972) *Character Analysis*, 3rd edn (edited by M. Higgins and C. Raphael). New York: Farrar, Straus and Giroux.

Richards, B. (1989) *Images of Freud: Cultural Responses to Psychoanalysis.* London: Weidenfeld Dent.

Richards, G. (1996) *Putting Psychology in Its Place: An Introduction from a Critical Historical Perspective.* London: Routledge.

Rose, N. (1985) *The Psychological Complex: Psychology, Politics and Society in England 1869–1939.* London: Routledge and Kegan Paul.

Rose, N. (1996) *Inventing Ourselves: Psychology, Power and Personhood.* Cambridge: Cambridge University Press.

Roudinesco, E. (1990) *Jacques Lacan and Co.: A History of Psychoanalysis in France, 1925–1985.* London: Free Association Books.

Sachs, W. (1996) *Black Hamlet*. Johannesburg: Witwatersrand University Press.

Samuels, A. (1993a) 'The mirror and the hammer: Depth psychology and political transformation', *Free Associations*, 3(4), 545–593.

Samuels, A. (1993b) *The Political Psyche.* London: Routledge.

Sarup, M. (1988) *An Introductory Guide to Post-structuralism and Postmodernism.* Hassocks, Sussex: Harvester Wheatsheaf.

Schmideberg, M. (1938) 'Intellectual inhibition and disturbances in eating', *International Journal of Psycho-Analysis*, 29, 17–22.

Schmideberg, M. (1971) 'A contribution to the history of the psycho-analytic movement in Britain', *The British Journal of Psychiatry,* 118, 61–68.

Shingu, K. (2004) *Being Irrational: Lacan, the Object, and the Golden Mean* (translated and edited by M. Radich). Tokyo: Gakuju Shoin.

Smith, J. (2004) 'Reflecting on the development of interpretative phenomenological analysis and its contribution to qualitative research in psychology', *Qualitative Research in Psychology,* 1, 39–54.

Smith, M.B. (1994) 'Selfhood at risk: Postmodern perils and the perils of postmodernism', *American Psychologist*, 49, 405–411.

Sodi, T. (1999) 'The meeting of a psychoanalyst and an indigenous healer', *Psychology in Society*, 25, 81–83.

Sokal, A. and Bricmont, J. (1998) *Intellectual Impostures: Postmodern Philosophers' Abuse of Science.* London: Profile Books.

Soler, C. (1996a) 'Transference', in R. Feldstein, B. Fink and M. Jaanus (eds) *Reading Seminars I and II: Lacan's Return to Freud.* New York: SUNY Press.

Soler, C. (1996b) 'Time and Interpret££ation', in R. Feldstein, B. Fink and M. Jaanus (eds) *Reading Seminars I and II: Lacan's Return to Freud.* New York: SUNY Press.

Solms, M. (2004) 'Is the brain more real than the mind?', in A. Casement (ed.) *Who Owns Psychoanalysis?* London: Karnac.

Squire, C. (1989) *Significant Differences: Feminism in Psychology.* London: Routledge.

Stern, D.N. (1985) *The Interpersonal World of the Infant: A View from Psychoanalysis and Developmental Psychology*. New York: Basic Books.

Straker, G. (1988) 'Child abuse, counselling and apartheid: The work of the Sanctuary Counselling Team', *Free Associations*, 14, 7–38.

Straker, G. (1994) 'The interface between refugee groups and assistance groups: An exploration of dynamics and the design of a treatment programme', *Free Associations*, 31, 320–327.

Symington, N. (1990) 'Religion and psychoanalysis', *Free Associations*, 19, 105–116.

Talvitie, V. and Ihanus, J. (2005) 'Biting the bullet: The nature of unconscious fantasy', *Theory & Psychology*, 15, 659–678.

Talvitie, V. and Tiitinen, H. (2006) 'From the repression of contents to the rules of the (narrative) self: A present-day cognitive view of the "Freudian phenomenon" of repressed contents', *Psychology and Psychotherapy: Theory, Research and Practice*, 79, 165–181.

Timms, E. and Segal, N. (eds) (1998) *Freud in Exile: Psychoanalysis and Its Vicissitudes.* New Haven and London: Yale University Press.

Trist, E. and Murray, H. (eds) (1990) *The Social Engagement of Social Science: A Tavistock Anthology: Vol. 1. The Socio-Psychological Perspective.* London: Free Association Books.

Voelklein, C. and Howarth, C. (2005) 'A review of controversies about social representations theory: A British debate', *Culture & Psychology*, 11, 431–454.

Waugaman, R.M. (1987) 'Falling off the couch', *Journal of the American Psychoanalytic Association*, 35, 861–876.

Westen, D., Novotny, C. and Thompson-Brenner, H. (2004) 'The empirical status of empirically supported psychotherapies: Assumptions, findings, and reporting in controlled clinical trials', *Psychological Bulletin*, 130(4), 631–663.

Wolfe, B. (1989) 'Diagnosis and distancing reactions', *Psychoanalytic Psychology*, 6(2), 187–198.

Wright, E. (1999) 'Transference: The impossible relation', *Psychoanalytic Studies*, 1(3), 263–267.

Young, R. (1993) 'Racism: Projective identification and cultural processes', *Psychology in Society*, 17, 5–18.

Žižek, S. (1989) *The Sublime Object of Ideology*. London: Verso.

Žižek, S. (1993a) 'Es gibt keinen Staat in Europa', in I. Arns (ed.) (2003) *Irwin: Retroprincip*. Frankfurt: Revolver.

Žižek, S. (1993b) 'Why are Laibach and NSK not Fascists?' In I. Arns (ed.) (2003) *Irwin: Retroprincip*. Frankfurt: Revolver.

Žižek, S. (1994) 'The enlightenment in Laibach'', in I. Arns (ed.) (2003) *Irwin: Retroprincip*. Frankfurt: Revolver.

Žižek, S. (2005) 'Foreword: They moved the underground', in A. Monroe (2005) *Interrogation Machine: Laibach and the NSK State*. Cambridge MA: MIT Press.

Index

www.ingramcontent.com/pod-product-compliance
Lightning Source LLC
La Vergne TN
LVHW021131300926
849160LV00010B/966